MAN TO MAN...
about God

THE LONDON
MEN'S CONVENTION
encouraging men to live for Christ

Man to Man… about God
© Christian Conventions 2008

Tel: 0845-225-0899
Fax: 0845-225-0898
email: admin@christianconventions.co.uk
www.christianconventions.co.uk

Published for The London Men's Convention by The Good Book Company
Elm House, 37 Elm Road, New Malden, Surrey KT3 3HB, UK.
Tel: 0845-225-0880
Fax: 0845-225-0990
email: admin@thegoodbook.co.uk

ISBN: 9781906334024

Cover design by Steve Devane

Printed in the UK by CPI Bookmarque, Croydon

CONTENTS

PREFACE

My friend Gordy is a professional musician. He's the drummer for a rock band and he spends a lot of time touring exotic places around the world. Gordy is very interested in Christianity but has lots of unanswered questions. Sometimes, when he's home, we train together at our local gym but, although we have great conversations, we rarely get the chance to get to grips with the heart of the Christian message. This is frustrating for both of us.

This book is for Gordy and other busy guys like him, who want to know what Jesus has to offer; to hear some hard evidence for faith in him, to hear sensible answers to the big questions about certainty, suffering and other religions, and to get past church traditions to the truth about Christ – in normal language.

It's a collection of great little talks for men from important parts of the Bible by experienced Bible teachers – speaking 'Man to Man... about God'.

This book is also for Christian men who want some ideas for explaining the Christian message clearly. It was published for the annual London Men's Convention which gathers men from churches all over south-east England into the prestigious surroundings of the Royal Albert Hall for encouragement to live for Christ. But the book is intended for men everywhere – sceptical, sympathetic and convinced alike – to help them know God.

Enjoy.

Richard Coekin
Chairman, the London Men's Convention

INTRODUCTION

It may seem strange that a book that aims to help men think more clearly about how God should be full of references to the Bible. What possible help could a 2000-year-old book be to modern men?

Many of us know some stories from the Bible, but, sadly, few of us have taken the trouble to seriously assess the Bible and its message as adults. We have vaguely heard that it is full of errors and untruths, and have moved on to other things.

The authors who contributed to this book have come to a different conclusion. Many of them started with similar suspicions about the relevance and reliability of the Bible, and yet, after careful study, now find themselves enthusiastic champions of its liberating message.

There's no space here to address these concerns in detail – there are many other excellent books that will help you sort out these questions. But as you read through this series of edited talks, we hope that you will begin to see that the Bible writers were wrestling with the same issues that so trouble 21st-century men. Despite the gap in culture, language and technology, they were still looking for answers to the questions we have: Where can I find meaning in life? How should I live? What makes a real man? What really matters in life?

It's worth remembering also that, despite rumours to the contrary, the Gospels – the accounts of Jesus' life in the Bible – are now recognised by most modern scholars as historically reliable for three reasons:

- **They are authentic history.** These are reliable versions of the original documents because so many copies were distributed throughout the Roman empire that errors in copying can easily be excluded and the original version identified. We can be confident that what we read in the Bible is what was originally written by their authors.

- **They are attested history.** These Gospel accounts of Jesus, and of other public figures of the period, like Pontius Pilate, Herod Agrippa, Caiaphas the High Priest and John the Baptist, are all confirmed by non-Christian writers of that time. We can be confident that this is not some made up story, but fits the facts as we know them from other sources.

- **They are accurate history.** These Gospel accounts are compiled from the eye-witness testimonies of those who actually met and heard Jesus. Indeed, Luke explains in his introduction that he carefully researched and selected records that will provide a reliable historical account. So we can be confident that what we read about Jesus gives us a reliable picture of what he was like, what he said, and what he did.

Perhaps you've been lent this book by a Christian friend, but would consider yourself to be sceptic. Can we urge you not to dismiss the Bible before you start, but rather to read this with an open mind? Discover and think about its message first. Remember that many of its writers were men like you, who found it just as hard to believe. And above all, take time to think about the central figure in the Bible – Jesus Christ – and why it is that he captivates the hearts and lives of so many men down the ages, and today.

Tim Thornborough
Editor

1 EMPTY PLEASURES

Hugh Palmer

I thought in my heart, "Come now, I will test you with pleasure to find out what is good." But that also proved to be meaningless. "Laughter," I said, "is foolish. And what does pleasure accomplish?" I tried cheering myself with wine, and embracing folly – my mind still guiding me with wisdom. I wanted to see what was worthwhile for men to do under heaven during the few days of their lives.

I undertook great projects: I built houses for myself and planted vineyards. I made gardens and parks and planted all kinds of fruit trees in them. I made reservoirs to water groves of flourishing trees. I bought male and female slaves and had other slaves who were born in my house. I also owned more herds and flocks than anyone in Jerusalem before me. I amassed silver and gold for myself, and the treasure of kings and provinces. I acquired men and women singers, and a harem as well – the delights of the heart of man. I became greater by far than anyone in Jerusalem before me. In all this my wisdom stayed with me.

I denied myself nothing my eyes desired;
I refused my heart no pleasure.
My heart took delight in all my work,
and this was the reward for all my labour.

Yet when I surveyed all that my hands had done
and what I had toiled to achieve,
everything was meaningless, a chasing after the wind;
nothing was gained under the sun.

ECCLESIASTES 2:1-11

2

In an age when tests and exams have multiplied enormously, and when you can get A-levels or degrees in subjects that had never been heard of in my day, here is one they missed out. Our school curriculum is still too limited because schools and universities don't offer a Masters in *'Pleasure'*. If they did, however, then the author of the book of Ecclesiastes, 'Mr Teacher' as he likes to call himself, would qualify for one.

Now the writer of Ecclesiastes might be 3,000 years old but he's so old that he's in fashion again. He invented the phrase, *'there's nothing new under the sun'*. He's made it his job to investigate life under the sun – life in here and now. In fact, this book is the blog of his experiences. He is trying to discover if there is any point to life but he doesn't leave us guessing very long. At the beginning of his second chapter he writes: 'I thought in my heart, "Come now, I will test you with pleasure to find out what is good." But that also proved to be meaningless.'

It's worth looking at his results in some detail, so let's examine this chapter and look at verses 2-10; the summary of his exhaustive pleasure research findings.

The research we'd all like to do

I did know someone once who managed to convince his university that he should spend three years researching the seashells of the Caribbean. Nice work if you can get it! Well, Mr Teacher goes one better. He is studying pleasure and he is more than happy to let his research take him wherever enjoyment might be found. He is committed to his pleasure research.

I don't know where you get your pleasure, but it's very likely that the Teacher has had a taste of it too. He begins with 'laughter' — the kind of laughter we'd call frivolity today: the fun of a game, a party, the office joker. Then he moves on to something he calls 'pleasure'. It's something just a little more upmarket than laughter; a touch more highbrow.

You know the type: the opera buff, the theatre-goer, the concert junkie. Next, he tries 'cheering myself with wine'. He joins in with the group that's always drowning their sorrows and drinking the evening away, either in the sophisticated wine bar or the local *Red Lion*. He calls it 'embracing folly' – the way in which some drown reality in a sea of joking and beer rather than face life as it is. They never think through their actions, just live for the next kick. It's the world of drugs or white-knuckle rides.

But whatever the Teacher puts himself through in the name of pleasure, he keeps his mind on his research, 'my mind still guiding me with wisdom'. All this is part of his analysis. He may have enjoyed the previous night's revelry, but when he gets up in the morning he still asks himself: *'Was it worth it?'*

Then there's the Teacher's creative side as well. Landscape gardening on a grand scale – 'I undertook great projects,' he says. 'I built houses for myself and planted vineyards. I made gardens and parks.' He's no half-hearted Bank Holiday gardener – he does it all.

By verse 7 he's acquired slaves; male and female. He has been on an intensive course of retail therapy. Born to shop. He's got many other slaves at home as well. And he's still amazingly wealthy.

> I owned more herds and flocks than anyone in Jerusalem before me.
> I amassed silver and gold for myself, and the treasure of kings and provinces.

With this kind of wealth at his disposal, we're not likely to be able to outdo him as a playboy.

In verse 8 he tells us that, *'I acquired men and women singers.'* He knew the power and attraction of music and enjoyed it to the full. If you are one of those who spends all day plugged in to an ipod, Mr Teacher will nod and say: 'I understand!'

Mr Teacher's pursuit of pleasure doesn't stop here though. By the end of verse 8 we can see he's got himself *'a harem as well — the delights of the hearts of men.'* He's had the wine and the song, and he makes sure he gets the women too. All the women a man could possibly want. It's said that Solomon – the King of Israel and the most likely writer of Ecclesiastes – had 700 wives and 300 concubines, which I think is more women than any man could possibly want! If sex is your thing, then Mr Teacher has been there, done that and got the T-shirt.

By verse 10 he tells us: *'I denied myself nothing my eyes desired.'* This was a very thorough piece of research. His diary is full of social engagements, his Blackberry crammed with numbers and emails for his clubs and contacts, and his credit-card holder is stretched to bursting. It's a no-expenses-spared experiment. Verse 10 is very striking: *'I refused my heart no pleasure.'* The Teacher carries no moral handcuffs. You name it? He's done it.

Remember the recent infamous Manchester United Christmas party? If the newspaper reports are to be believed, they hired a hotel exclusively for themselves. The players contributed £4000 each, invited 100 selected women from all over the place, but no wives, no girlfriends and all mobile phones taken away at the door. Mr Teacher understands that kind of a party.

He's thrilled to be doing this research. So let's pay very close attention as he comes to his conclusion. It's not me, the boring middle-aged rector having his say. It's not a tirade against sin and pleasure from someone who makes you wonder if he really knows what any of those things are actually like. No, this verdict is from a man we'd better listen to, because, when he finishes his pleasure research, he supplies us with his conclusions in verse 11.

The morning after the night before!

Verse 11 has got that kind of feel to it when we look at it; we come down to earth with a bump. After all that heady excitement, Mr Teacher's verdict leaves life very flat indeed.

> Yet when I surveyed all that my hands had done and what I had toiled to achieve, everything was meaningless, a chasing after the wind; nothing was gained under the sun.

He gets up and looks into the mirror in the cold light of day. He has the guts to look life straight in the eye, examine his liver and face the facts. He's not content just to put a brave face on it – that's what makes him truly wise. His big question, which he raised in his first chapter was: *'What does man gain from all his labour at which he toils under the sun?'* and here he answers it. *'Nothing was gained under the sun.'* What's the profit? Meaningless.

'A chasing after the wind.' Ever tried doing that? Complete waste of time, isn't it? We can run as long and as fast as we like but we'll never catch it. Empty. The sense is never satisfied.

Oh yes, there are fleeting moments of triumph, but they are all too brief. Fifteen minutes of fame, but then what? The *Big Brother* celebrities who live out the rest of their lives as increasingly meaningless items in the tabloid newspapers.

The years go by all too quickly, the creative juices dry up, the body bulges where it shouldn't and the victories are harder to come by. The joy was in the toil: *'My heart took delight in all my work.'* The thrill was in the chase. He loved making the conquests, but once he had completed things... *meaningless.*

Actually, we don't really need Mr Teacher to tell us that. Others have discovered the truth from their own bitter experience. Jack Higgins, the author of *The Eagle has Landed* and many other novels, was once asked in an interview: 'Is there anything you wish someone had told you before you set out on all this success?' And he replied:

> Yes. I wish someone had told me that when you get to the top there's nothing there.

It's chasing after the wind.

Pop stars' lives seem to shout it out at times. Everyone from Elvis to Britney Spears. Here's what Kurt Cobain of Nirvana wrote in his suicide note:

> I haven't felt the excitement of listening to as well as creating music for too many years now. I can't stand the thought of Frances [his daughter] becoming the miserable, self-destructive death rocker that I've become.

Everything was meaningless.

Or go back to a big name from my youth, the great comedian Tony Hancock. In the sixties, over 15 million people – 30% of the adult population in the UK – used to tune in each week to *Hancock's Half Hour*. He reduced the nation to tears of laughter. He was a superb artist and comic but, in 1968, he committed suicide. Not long before his death, he included these lines in a monologue on a show talking of his death and what to put on his gravestone.

'E came, 'e went, in between, nothing. Won't even notice he's gone. One day in the pub someone will say, "Where's old Hancock? Haven't seen him recently." "Oh, Hancock? He's dead."

He had talked long with friends about the meaning and purpose of life but had refused to accept any answers. Spike Milligan, another great comedian, knew him well and said this:

'One by one he shut the door on all the people he knew, and then he shut the door on himself.'

So much for laughter.

Mr Teacher says: 'Chase all of this if you want, but we must face the post-mortem; the morning after the night before.' It's not guilty feelings he talks about here. He speaks of something even more profound; he says it doesn't work. We can play life hard and fast – as if there are no rules if we like – but we'll find there is on:; it doesn't deliver.

I don't know about you, but I can only take so much of this. There comes a time when I want to say to Mr Teacher: *'Ok, I won't argue with you anymore. Stop all the negatives, will you? Tell me what you do suggest!'* But Mr Teacher won't even let us get to his recommendations very quickly because he knows that, for some of us, our work is our pleasure… not for Mr Teacher though. He's all too conscious about where a life lived for work leads, or rather, where it doesn't lead. In chapter two, verse 17, he states:

So I hated life, because the work that is done under the sun was grievous to me. All of it is meaningless, a chasing after the wind. I hated all the things I had toiled for under the sun because I must leave them to the one who comes after me. And who knows whether he will be a wise man or a fool? Yet he will have control over

> all the work into which I have poured my effort and skill under the
> sun. This too is meaningless.

Where's all the work going?

John D Rockefeller, from that extremely wealthy American family, apparently had an income of about $1 million a week towards the end of his life. But his doctors only allowed him to eat the barest minimum, so he lived on a diet that a pauper would have hated. One of his biographers described it like this:

> Now less than 100 pounds in weight, he sampled everything at
> breakfast: a drop of coffee, a spoonful of cereal, a forkful of egg, and
> a bit of chop the size of a pea.

The richest man in the world but he couldn't even enjoy his food.

As for Mr Teacher, the thought of death is never far away either. Recently, I took my family to the British Museum to visit the remarkable exhibition of 'The First Emperor' and his astonishing terracotta army. It was packed but well worth the visit.

That first emperor was a remarkable man. From his home in the one state of Chin, within nine years he had conquered the rest of China, built 270 palaces and pulled the whole nation together. More than 30 years before he died, he was preparing his tomb because he saw himself not only as emperor of all of this world, but also the emperor of the whole of the afterlife. They buried him and, in 1974, someone stumbled upon the head from one of the terracotta soldiers. They found 7000 life-size model soldiers buried with him, guarding him. Extraordinary, isn't it?

However, within four years of his death, his dynasty had come to an end in China and was replaced. And these days, you can speak to anyone who has been to the exhibition and they'll tell you all about the soldiers, but I should think very few will be able to tell you what his name was. He's more famous for his model soldiers than himself.

That's the trouble with death, isn't it? *'Like the fool,'* our Teacher says in verse 16, *'the wise man too must die!'* Meaningless ... chasing after the wind.

You might be thinking to yourself: 'Look I've heard you. I get the message. It's a waste of time. I'm feeling down, but I've got the rest of my life ahead. What do you suggest Mr Teacher?' Well, he shares his conclusions with us in verses 24-26 and, for the first time, it seems as if there might be a ray of light in this gloomy picture.

Mr Teacher gets positive

Mr Teacher's first flash of hope is that he doesn't believe we live in a closed world. He doesn't actually believe that 'life under the sun' is all there is. It's why he won't even let me enjoy that threadbare philosophy of 'eat, drink and be merry, for tomorrow we die.' But he's not a killjoy either. He doesn't say we have to join a monastery to be godly and find meaning. There are real pleasure possibilities in this life.

Look at verse 24:

> A man can do nothing better than to eat and drink and find satisfaction in his work. This too, I see, is from the hand of God, for without him, who can eat or find enjoyment?

To eat, to drink, to find satisfaction; these things are good. These pleasures can be enjoyed if we don't put a weight on them which is too much for them to bear. If we don't live for our work, our art, our food or our sport; if we don't make idols of them, they can bring us God-given contentment.

And, for a brief second, it's as if the Teacher has pulled back the curtain:

> To the man who pleases him, God gives wisdom, knowledge and happiness.

It's just a glimpse but he's in no rush to give us hasty answers. And Christians sometimes need to learn from him. Some of us can get to the stage where it seems we can't say anything without everything coming out. A friend once told me about a visit in Rwanda. He spoke of one young man who became a Christian and, a few days later, was at an open-air meeting. A friend of his spotted him at the meeting, ran up to him and asked: *'What's it all about?'* The young Christian just turned to his friend and said: *'Oh how I wish you knew'* and left it there! A few weeks later the friend was so intrigued, he went and found out for himself and became a Christian too.

It reminded me of a comment I read in the paper recently.

> I was standing in the queue at midnight, waiting with my daughter to buy a copy of the last Harry Potter book. It was cold and I was tired, and there was a man offering hot coffee at a stall near by. How enterprising, I thought. I went over to get a coffee. 'How much?' I asked. 'It's free,' the man replied. Looking down, I noticed a flyer for a Christian group on the stall. 'But you want some sort of donation, right?' 'No,' said the man, 'it's free.' 'Why would you give coffee away for free? What's in it for you?' I asked. The man just smiled. I took my free coffee. I've often thought about that smile, trying to figure it out.

I think Mr Teacher would have enjoyed that smile.

The greater teacher

Hundreds of years after Mr Teacher finished his book, an even greater teacher came. He came with the astonishing offer of a life that keeps on satisfying. We can read what he says in chapter four of John's Gospel. We find this teacher talking to a woman who's stumbled from one broken relationship to another. She's gone through five husbands and she's with yet another man. He says this to her:

> Jesus answered, "Everyone who drinks this water will be thirsty again, but whoever drinks the water I give him will never thirst. Indeed, the water I give him will become in him a spring of water welling up to eternal life."

Malcolm Muggeridge was a very powerful, if somewhat intellectual, television personality. He became a Christian towards the end of his life and he said this:

> I may, I suppose, regard myself or pass for being a relatively successful man. People occasionally stare at me in the streets – that's fame. I can fairly easily earn enough to qualify for admission to the higher

slopes of the Inland Revenue – that's success. Furnished with money and a little fame, even the elderly, if they care to, may partake of trendy diversions – that's pleasure. It might happen once in a while that something I said or wrote was sufficiently heeded for me to persuade myself that it represented a serious impact on our time – that's fulfilment. Yet I say to you, and I beg you to believe me, multiply those tiny triumphs by a million, add them all together and they're nothing, less than nothing, measured against one draught of that living water Christ offers to the spiritually thirsty irrespective of who or what they are.

The water I give him will become in him a spring of water welling up to eternal life,' said Jesus. In chapter 10 of John's Gospel we can see this teacher, Jesus, saying something even more striking. He claims to bring life *without spin*. That's a welcome relief for anyone who has glimpsed this sense of meaningless and is looking for real answers. Hear what he says in verse 10 of chapter 10:

The thief comes only to steal and kill and destroy; I have come that they may have life, and have it to the full.

Nicholas Bengli was a Zulu evangelist who said:

I'd been looking for joy and the devil gave me fun. I'd been looking for peace and the devil gave me error. I'd been looking for experience and the devil gave me excitement. Then I found Christ.

'I have come that they may have life, and have it to the full.' You ask: 'What's that all about?'

How I wish you knew...

2 HOW TO BE A REAL MAN
Tim Thornborough

Imagine for a moment what a Martian student would think if he took a trip to earth to research an essay on *'Men – what are they and what makes them tick?'* What do we look like from the outside? What conclusions would he reach about us as a whole?

He might drop in to a local newsagent before doing some observational field research to look at some of the things men are interested in reading about. A quick trawl through the shelves for men reveals a complex variety of subjects. Men, it would seem, are interested in sex, cars, sex, computers, sex, body building, more sex and clothes... and did I mention sex?

But dig a little deeper, and the magazines would tell him that the only reason that men are interested in cars, body building and clothes is so that they can have more... you guessed it... sex!

I'm not quite sure where computers fit in.

In search of the real man
The question of men's identity is something that is deeply felt by men and women alike. And the magazines are not slow to give suggestions for how we should answer the question: 'What makes a real man?'

All the girls say that it's what they're searching for: 'a real man.' And meanwhile we poor men are scratching our heads for longer and longer, wondering if it's possible to make our minds up about what that is. We're told we have to be loving and sensitive and caring. We're told that the old caveman is now out of fashion. We're told that we have to get more involved with the housework, and be more 'relational'. But deep down, we suspect that this is simply women re-inventing us. As the ad on the tube says: 'Women want a man who will hold their hand and their shopping.'

So there's been a monster backlash. Top-shelf magazines are no longer on the top shelf. And macho maleness is back on the agenda. The popular magazines carry this message for men. So long as you pump iron and get a great body; so long as you dress smart and cool; so long as you work hard and/or 'smart' and make loads of cash, then the world is your playground.

Trouble is, I didn't think grown men were supposed to spend their time in the playground... isn't that for children?

Some suggestions

So what is a real man – a genuine human being of the male variety? Let's look at some of the suggestions you'll find in the popular magazines.

Your body

The adverts show moody-looking guys with a six-pack stomach and bulging biceps. The gym membership is the way to achieve it.

But it seems to me that all that banging and thumping away on a treadmill turns you, not so much into a human being, as into something that more resembles a hamster.

The gym I joined a couple of years ago gave me some target vital statistics for my age, height and body shape. When I looked at the numbers, I felt quite depressed until I came up with a way to achieve them instantly – by swapping where they were supposed to be. It was the only way I could possibly hope to make a success of it.

Don't get me wrong – it's great to be strong and fit and healthy. And there's no doubt that looking good can make you feel good and more confident about yourself. But it only takes a moment's thought to know that this can't be the answer to our question. We are not just bodies. We all instinctively know that there is more to our lives than this.

As a friend of mine says, exercise won't make you live any forever – you'll just look a much better corpse on the slab.

Your work

This is often the label that blokes use to describe themselves. 'I'm a teacher. What do you do?' 'I'm a plumber – £50 please'. It's a convenient way to pigeonhole others and to feel important about yourself. And there is also a massive amount we can achieve through our work.

You may be someone who lives to work, or you could be someone who works to live. But whichever you are, the limitations of this approach to understanding ourselves should be obvious. Are we saying that people who have retired are no longer human? And are we saying that people with lowly, boring or mindless jobs are any less human than those whose jobs are more impressive?

Work is really important, but it surely cannot be how we define ourselves. That's defining a *Human Doing,* not a *Human Being.*

Your wealth

I'm not just talking about salary, stocks, shares, saving accounts, ISAs, mini-ISAs, mini cash-ISAs and the like. But also what you own – the house, the computer, the iPod, the TV, the car. These are the status symbols by which we judge our own success and value, and also by which we judge others.

We gamble, we work, we strive to fill our lives with pretty, comfortable things, and to afford the best that life has to offer. But what does it mean at the end of the day? Of course, money *does* make you happy – or at least, happier than you would be if you had nothing. But money doesn't necessarily make you *fulfilled*, unless you're particularly shallow.

Having stuff can be a lot of fun, and poverty is a terrible thing, but, as the saying goes, there are no pockets in a shroud. You can't take it with you. And it only takes a second's thought to realise that 'the one with the most money at the end of the game wins' is a ridiculous way to live your life. Because the end of the game for us is to be put in a box in the ground, or else a quick trip up the crematory chimney.

Providing for yourself and others is really important, but surely it shouldn't be how we define ourselves. That's defining a *Human Having,* not a *Human Being.*

Your relationships

When we get to the subject of relationships, I suspect that we get a little nearer to the truth about what makes a real man.

Most blokes I know are in denial about the 'R' word – we'd rather be married than be in a relationship. But in its broadest sense, we get nearer to the mark of what a real man is and should be when we think about how we live and see ourselves – as sons and brothers – as friends and team-mates – as husbands and fathers.

When these relationships are good, then life is good. And whatever life throws at you, you can manage it. But when family or friends or lovers are bad, then life can seem hardly worth living at all, and the smallest thing can make us fly off the handle or just crumple.

But is there any lasting value in these things? Is it enough for me to be able to say at the end of a long life that I've been a good dad and a faithful husband? Is it enough to know that my memory will live on in the lives I have touched and been part of? Is this the legacy that counts for a real man – to love and to have been loved? Many of us would think so, but, at the same time would be painfully aware that we have failed repeatedly in all these areas. We have been more concerned about ourselves than others; we have let friends down; we have betrayed our lovers and failed in our responsibilities to those who depend on us. It's not hard to make men feel guilty – because if we take the trouble to look at ourselves, yes, we see things we like. But at the same time, we find aspects to our lives that make us blush with shame.

Why, we ask, do we have this sense of what is right and good, of what we should aspire to as men, and yet at the same time, an unfailing tendency to mess it up?

Understanding why

The Bible proposes an extraordinary answer to this deep question of who we are. On the very first page of the Bible we find this statement:

> So God created man in his own image, in the image of God he created him; male and female he created them. **Genesis 1:27**

Human beings, the Bible claims, are not the result of a random accident, but the result of God's intelligent and creative will.

Many of us spend our time looking at sportsmen, heroes or role models – people we want to be like. The Bible writers tell us that we already look like someone – God! He made us in His image. I don't think that means a physical resemblance. It has something to do with the kind of bloke I am – the way I am in my character and relationships. He made me to love and laugh and create and relate. And just as he delighted in his creation, so we, in God's image, were made to delight and enjoy the world he has put us in.

To put it the other way round, it means that I should be able to look at anyone and say: *'God is like that!'* I should be able to observe your creativity, your sense of right and wrong, your delight in beauty and good things, your love and commitment to others, your responsible care of friends, wives and children, and see a perfect reflection of the God who made you. Because He is all those things, and so much more.

But the tragedy is that we don't see this at all. We see flashes of all those things, but they are often the exception to a different daily reality – of self- centred indifference, idleness and misplaced pride. It's not that many of us are involved in stuff that you would describe as 'evil'. For most of us, it's just the low-level, day-by-day experience of living for ourselves. Of making choices that suit us and feed our ego, rather than giving ourselves to others.

What went wrong?

We were made in the image of God. But as the story of mankind unfolds in the Bible, we discover the reason that this image of God's goodness and life in us has been defaced. We have tried to push God out of our lives. We have put ourselves at the centre of things instead of Him. We have rejected the right way of living in God's world, and chosen to make our own way instead.

The opening chapters of the Bible explain this 'fall' and its consequences in the story of Adam and Eve – the first man and woman. They enjoyed God's generosity and friendship, but rejected God's authority over them. Their desire to reject God had, and still has, awful consequences, because God is not neutral about this spoiling of his creation. He will hold us to account for what we have done to ourselves and others. The penalty for this rebellion is death.

I was thrilled when I heard my wife describe me to a friend as a model huband. Until I looked it up the word 'model' in the dictionary, where it said: *A small plastic imitation of the real thing*. And the Bible says that this is what we have become through rejecting God. Some cheap substitute for the real thing. And at the end of the day, God will consign this cheap substitute to the place it belongs – the waste bin. How can we escape this terrible fate?

How can we find the way back to being a real man? If only we could find someone who hadn't fallen. Someone who would be a true model for what we are supposed to be. Someone who would give us a true view of what a man should be!

The real man

And so the Bible's story reaches its massive climax with angels singing in the sky as a long-promised child is born into the world. Jesus would be God's answer to all our questions.

His life was everything that ours are not. Filled with compassion for the weak and helpless. Tirelessly giving of himself to all comers. Condemning the hypocrisy of the religious leaders of the day. Challenging injustice wherever his piercing gaze met it. And all without a thought for his own reputation, safety and comfort. This amazing life is one reason why his followers became convinced that his claims were true. The apostle Paul wrote of Jesus later;

He is the image of the invisible God, the firstborn over all creation.

Colossians 1:15

The image of God! In other words, look at Jesus the God-Man and you discover three things:

- What God is like – he is God's image.
- What a real man should be like – we were made in God's image, but are fallen
- How much you fall below the standard

The problem is that we spend our time comparing ourselves with each other. There are some exceptional people around that we would all want to be like – in looks, physique, intelligence, abilities or the amount of cash in their pockets. But when we compare our true selves, our character and passions with each other, we're pretty much the same. Of course there are some completely rubbish people that we look down on. Murderers, rapists, politicians – people like that. And there's the occasional great man we look up to.

But when we compare ourselves with Jesus, we see what a catastrophe our lives really are. We discover that we have been fooling ourselves when we think we are 'alright.' We find that even our best moments are shot through with selfish motives and glory-seeking.

When someone holds up a mirror to your life like that, it might be painful, but they are doing you a favour. They are helping us see reality – what we are truly like. But rather than humbly admit our mistakes, we took the other solution. When Jesus walked among us, it was as if he was holding up a mirror that revealed our true selves. We should have been grateful to receive the truth, but we did something else.

We smashed the mirror.

His beautiful life was destroyed because it showed how broken we really are. Jesus was betrayed, convicted, crucified and killed because he told the truth – he was the truth – about God, about humanity, and about you and me. He lived the life we could not hope to live. But it meant that the death he died was able to achieve something extraordinary.

In the brilliant plan of God, even this ultimate act of rebellion – murdering our creator – was part of his plan to put us right with him.

> God was pleased to reconcile to himself all things ... by making peace through his blood, shed on the cross. **Colossians 1:20**

In the very death of Jesus, God made it possible for weak and ruined men to be at peace with God. He has given the very people who are his enemies the opportunity to become his friends.

And God offers to each of us the opportunity to start again in a new life with Jesus as our Lord. It's a life that is built on the right foundation, so that, at last, we can start to become real men, who are being re-created in the image of our loving God.

I used to work as a journalist in the Middle East, and would sometimes get invited to fancy parties. Once, when I was in the Jordanian capital, Amman, I went with a friend to a party at the Indian Embassy. It was a cold night, and, unusually, it was even snowing. As I arrived at the entrance to the grand building, a hilarious sight met my eyes. By the door stood a man with an enormous beard and moustache, dressed in the most outlandish clothes I had ever seen in my life. Gold shoes that curled up at the end. A red and green richly embroidered jacket and trousers. And all topped off with a huge puffy hat like an enormous round cushion. He looked like something out of the Arabian nights. I was laughing so much at the sight that as I handed this ridiculous-looking doorman my coat, I took off my hat and plopped it on top of his before swishing into the reception.

My friend leaned over to me and whispered hoarsely: 'You've just put your hat on top of the Indian Ambassador!'

I could have died on the spot.

I suspect it's like that for many of us with Jesus. We've not really treated him as we ought to. We've made ourselves at home in his place, drunk his champagne, eaten from the generous buffet table, but failed to honour him as we should. Most of the time we haven't even had the common decency to say thank you.

That night at the Embassy, I should have gone back to the man I'd insulted and asked his forgiveness. I should have said to him: 'I'm most terribly sorry; I didn't realise who you are. Do you have it in your heart to forgive me?'

We need to come to Jesus the same way. Humbly saying sorry for the mess we have made of the life he has given to us. And the truly wonderful thing is that he doesn't push us away as we deserve. Nor does he condemn us as he has every right to. Rather, he is able to say to us: 'Yes, I will forgive you. I *can* forgive you, because of my death on the cross.'

Sad to say, that night at the embassy, I took the coward's way out. I slipped off into the night, too cowardly and embarrassed to make my apology.

Make sure you don't do that with Jesus. The consequences are far more costly, the implications far more important for this world and the next.

Instead, *be a man*. Face up to the reality of what you really are, and come face to face with the real man – Jesus Christ, who lived the life you ought to lead. And died a death for you.

Because not only will He give you a fresh start in life, with all your past failures forgiven, but he'll also teach you how to be a real man, and give you the strength to become one.

3 THE PRODIGAL SON

Roger Carswell

Jesus continued: 'There was a man who had two sons. The younger one said to his father, "Father, give me my share of the estate." So he divided his property between them.

'Not long after that, the younger son got together all he had, set off for a distant country and there squandered his wealth in wild living. After he had spent everything, there was a severe famine in that whole country, and he began to be in need. So he went and hired himself out to a citizen of that country, who sent him to his fields to feed pigs. He longed to fill his stomach with the pods that the pigs were eating, but no one gave him anything.

'When he came to his senses, he said, "How many of my father's hired men have food to spare, and here I am starving to death! I will set out and go back to my father and say to him: 'Father, I have sinned against heaven and against you. I am no longer worthy to be called your son; make me like one of your hired men.'" So he got up and went to his father.

'But while he was still a long way off, his father saw him and was filled with compassion for him; he ran to his son, threw his arms around him and kissed him.

'The son said to him, "Father, I have sinned against heaven and against you. I am no longer worthy to be called your son."

'But the father said to his servants, "Quick! Bring the best robe and put it on him. Put a ring on his finger and sandals on his feet. Bring the fattened calf and kill it. Let's have a feast and celebrate. For this son of mine was dead and is alive again; he was lost and is found." So they began to celebrate.

'Meanwhile, the older son was in the field. When he came near the house, he heard music and dancing. So he called one of the servants and asked him what was going on. "Your brother has come," he replied, "and your father has killed the fattened calf because he has him back safe and sound."

'The older brother became angry and refused to go in. So his father went out and pleaded with him. But he answered his father, "Look! All these years I've been slaving for you and never disobeyed your orders. Yet you never gave me even a young goat so I could celebrate with my friends. But when this son of yours who has squandered your property with prostitutes comes home, you kill the fattened calf for him!"

'"My son," the father said, "you are always with me, and everything I have is yours. But we had to celebrate and be glad, because this brother of yours was dead and is alive again; he was lost and is found."'

LUKE 15:11-32

Nothing has the power to capture men's imagination as much as a good story, and there is no better one than that told by Jesus in his parable of *The Prodigal Son*. In Germany, looking at it from the other angle, they call it *The Parable of the Waiting Father*. The story rings true; it has the marks of authenticity about it; it reflects the experience of many families – perhaps even your own.

History is full of stories of good and even godly homes which have experienced the bitterness and grief of one or more of their children becoming wayward. The heartache and disappointment this brings to caring parents has to be felt to be understood.

Let's examine Jesus' story in three stages.

The son 'left home' before he left home

Outwardly, no doubt, everything looked fine. The father and his two sons worked their land, tended their animals and appeared prosperous and united. Inwardly though, the second-born son was tormented with the tedium of home. Within him there dwelt a cry for freedom. He knew about the bright lights of the big city and he wanted to live without restraint.

Of course, everything he had came from his father — his very being, possessions, security and prospects — but he wasn't focusing on these. As people brought up in the country want to live in the city, so city people want to live in the country. He was a country boy and longed for the city.

While tilling the ground, he dreamt of being away from it. His heart was away from home even if he hadn't escaped yet.

Eventually, he plucked up the courage to approach his father. His tone expressed his feelings. 'Give me,' he said, and what else could the father do other than give the inheritance which his son would eventually have? Within days, his bags were packed, and he walked out through the door towards his dream.

So often the real person who God has created is hijacked by a cruel understudy. What they are and should be become slaves to un realistic and foolish ideas about themselves, and what will make them happy. This is what happened here.

The son was entirely responsible for his actions; he wilfully turned his back on his home and its values; he willingly joined himself to 'a distant country'. He had developed a taste for a lifestyle that was contrary to both his father's and, more importantly, God's.

For a while life was new but, in time, it was to prove a disappointing way of life. For a while it was all he had ever dreamed of; there were pleasures in sin, though only for a short time. While he had the money, he had fun. Life was sweet, friends were numerous and the world was his oyster.

Though he now lived the life he had longed for back on his father's farm, he struggled with a basic disappointment in his heart and mind. A nagging feeling of doubt that only grew as he saw the numbers on his bank statement drop lower and lower.

And to make matters worse, just as his money ran out, a famine hit the land with devastating consequences. Desperate to find employment, he took a job looking after pigs. You can almost hear the gasp from the Jewish people who first heard this story from the lips of Jesus. Looking after these 'unclean' animals that they would never have touched marks the lowest point possible for a human being to go. For the son, it was the lowest of the low – it was the end point of his prodigal living.

The son 'returned home' before he returned home

He was so desperately poor that he longed to eat the food that his pigs were given, just to avoid starvation. All his long-held dreams were shattered. He began to see for himself the truth of the Bible's wise statement that 'the way of sinners' is hard.

He began to recall the days when life seemed so secure and pleasant; when he never had to wonder where his next meal was coming from, nor struggle with an accusing conscience and the scars of wrong living. He remembered the better times he had known with his father. He tried to recall his father's character and imagine what his father's reaction would be if he dared to return home.

We are not told, but I suppose the intense struggle lasted for weeks. A sense of emptiness, hunger and disappointment doing battle in his mind with the humiliation of returning and the risk of rejection.

It reminds me of Fyodor Dostoevsky (1821–81), the Russian novelist who wrote *Crime and Punishment* and *The Brothers Karamazov*. Brought up in a God-fearing home in the 1820s, he turned his back on the faith and dignity of his parents and became involved in radical political activities. When a new Tsar (the Russian King) came to power, however, he was arrested, tried for treason and sentenced to death.

Moments before his public execution, he was granted a reprieve and marched hundreds of miles to serve for years in a Siberian labour camp. Just before entering the prison, from which he would not emerge for a decade, a woman came up to him and gave him a parcel in which were a few roubles and a Russian Bible. During his prison sentence, he repeatedly read the Bible, but it wasn't until some time later that he actually came to the point where he became a Christian.

In his mind, he was convinced of the truth of Christianity as he read the Bible, but it took a long time for his heart to be willing to submit to the claims of Christ.

I am sure that the prodigal son was similar – and his was the experience of many, perhaps even you reading this now. Many people know the truth of the gospel of Christ and have experienced the void and lack of freedom that comes though rejecting him, but spend perhaps years unwilling to yield to the lordship of Jesus in their lives.

Jesus taught the need to repent, which in the Bible simply means to change your mind about what is really important. The reason Jesus calls us to repent is twofold. He lovingly warns us to *'repent or you will go to hell'*. In other words, you must change your mind on these things, because the consequences are disastrous if you remain where you are. But more often he says that we must: *'repent for the kingdom of heaven is at hand'*. In other words, you must make up your mind about this, or you will miss out on the most fabulous prize possible – eternal life. And time is running out.

He was 'welcomed home' before he arrived home

The hardest step for the prodigal was the first one. To actually pick himself up to leave the pig farm and set off back was the biggest decision of his life. No doubt the hunger, the threat of starvation and his disgust with his present situation drove him out of his pigsty. But what drew him to home was not just the thought of food and a warm bed. He was reckoning on the goodness of his father to welcome him.

When he had left home, he had everything; now, returning, he had nothing. He tried to work through what he would say to his father. Recognising that all sin is first and foremost against God, he prepared his speech: *'Father, I have sinned against heaven and against you. I am no longer worthy to be called your son.'* The *'give me'* he had spoken to his father when he left, now became *'make me'*. As he plodded down the road to home rehearsing this speech, his mind must have filled with fear about what his father would say. Would he be filled with accusations? *'How dare you darken my door!'* Or would he be angry at the insult to his reputation and honour?

His father, however, had been longing for this day. If he had lived today, he would have sent letters, cards, emails and faxes to his son. By any means, he wanted his son to know that he would be welcome home with *absolutely no strings attached*. Maybe he was sitting on the flat roof of his middle-eastern house looking to the distant horizon, waiting to see his son. The daily disappointment he had endured did not kill the sense of expectation he had.

And, when he saw a little cloud of dust in the distance, he screwed up his eyes, wondering if this could be his lost son. When he saw what appeared to be a familiar figure, he pulled his robe up to his knees, scurried down the steps at the side of the house and ran to welcome him.

If the villagers shouted: 'Leave him! Don't forget what he's done to you!', this father was not listening. He had waited so longingly, and now he welcomed his son so lovingly. The son started on his prepared speech but was cut short by the suffocating embrace of his tearful father. The sheer exuberance and excitement at welcoming home his long-lost son completely overwhelmed him.

No doubt news of how his son had lived had reached his father, but there were no questions asked. The fact that his son was repentant and home was sufficient.

The law of the day decreed that a son who had behaved in such a manner could be punished by stoning. But if anyone had tried, the stones would have just hit his father, who had his arms around his son.

How God accepts us

Abraham Lincoln, after his victory in the American Civil War, was asked: *'How shall we treat the defeated Southerners?'* He replied: *'We'll treat them as if they had never been away.'* The father's attitude in Jesus' story is the same.

It is a picture of the love of God. The father was rich in mercy. This is a story, not of rags to riches, but of rags to righteousness. In other words, God accepts prodigals back to himself, not grudgingly, or with any sense that they need to 'make up' for what they have done, but as though they had never been away. God's forgiveness is so complete that it is as though we had never done anything at all. That love which rushes to welcome us is only possible because the price has already been paid when Christ died for us.

Jesus, who told this parable, knew that he was going to a place called Calvary, where He would suffer and die, paying the price of the sin of the world. The sin of our wasteful living was laid on Jesus on the cross. He died to set us free and to forgive us for everything in our lives that defies God.

Raising Jesus from the dead three days later, God demonstrated that he had accepted what Christ had accomplished in his death. Jesus had obtained for his followers freedom from their sin and death. His power to defeat this, life's greatest enemy, was evident.

The elder brother was to criticise what the father did, but the father felt that his son, who had been dead and lost to him, was now found and alive. A new robe and sandals were found. He had a ring placed on his finger and the best calf was ordered to be killed for the joyful celebration.

All that the son had hoped for in the distant country, he now had at home in his the joy and security of his father. He was accepted because of the father's great love for him, rather than for what he possessed or did.

Why God allows us to walk out on him is beyond our comprehension. But he does.

The author C S Lewis once wrote about a similarly dysfunctional family. ' *"Dad, I'm not at all sure I can follow you any longer in your simple Christian faith,"* said the clergyman's son, when he returned from the university for the holidays with a fledgling scholar's assured arrogance. The father's black eyes skewered his young son, who was lost in the invincible ignorance of his intellect.

"Son", the father said, *"that is your freedom. Your terrible freedom".* '

And why God should so freely welcome us back is, again, more than our understanding can grasp. But his love and willingness to forgive is infinite and, whoever we are, whatever we have done, wherever we have been, God is willing to give a warm welcome and a fresh start. We cannot come to him as we like — there has to be an attitude of sorrow and willingness to turn from our sin — but he will take us as we are. Then he doesn't leave us as we are. He makes all things new. He begins the process of preparing us to be happy with Him for all eternity.

The invitation and welcome are there. The issue is whether you will return to God, turning from all that is wrong, and trusting Him to be the loving Lord over your future, both in life and eternity.

4 THE DYING THIEF

John Tindall

As they led him away, they seized Simon from Cyrene, who was on his way in from the country, and put the cross on him and made him carry it behind Jesus. A large number of people followed him, including women who mourned and wailed for him. Jesus turned and said to them, "Daughters of Jerusalem, do not weep for me; weep for yourselves and for your children. For the time will come when you will say, 'Blessed are the barren women, the wombs that never bore and the breasts that never nursed!' Then " 'they will say to the mountains, "Fall on us!" and to the hills, "Cover us!" ' For if men do these things when the tree is green, what will happen when it is dry?"

Two other men, both criminals, were also led out with him to be executed. When they came to the place called the Skull, there they crucified him, along with the criminals—one on his right, the other on his left. Jesus said, "Father, forgive them, for they do not know what they are doing." And they divided up his clothes by casting lots. The people stood watching, and the rulers even sneered at him. They said, "He saved others; let him save himself if he is the Christ of God, the Chosen One."

The soldiers also came up and mocked him. They offered him wine vinegar and said, "If you are the king of the Jews, save yourself." There was a written notice above him, which read: THIS IS THE KING OF THE JEWS.

One of the criminals who hung there hurled insults at him: "Aren't you the Christ? Save yourself and us!" But the other criminal rebuked him. "Don't you fear God," he said, "since you are under the same sentence? We are punished justly, for we are getting what our deeds deserve. But this man has done nothing wrong."

Then he said, "Jesus, remember me when you come into your kingdom." Jesus answered him, "I tell you the truth, today you will be with me in paradise."

LUKE 23: 26-43

I didn't sleep much last night, I was too worried about what was going to happen today. I did drift off eventually but I woke up with the rising sun streaming through a small hole in the wall. I remembered in one sickening moment that it was to be the last time I would wake up. It would be the last time I'd see a sunrise. Today I'm going to be taken through the streets of the city carrying a large piece of timber. I'll arrive at a place outside the wall of the city and by 9:00 I'll be nailed to that lump of wood.

I can't imagine what horrible things I'll experience – I've seen it before. I'll hang there naked in the hot sun for hours. If I'm not dead by sunset, they'll come and break my legs with a hammer so that I'll choke to death under the weight of my own body. Tomorrow is the Sabbath and they won't leave me there on their holy day.

I wish, now, I hadn't started on a life of crime. Robbing people seemed an easy way of making ends meet. I've managed to harden my heart and shut out the voice of conscience. But now that the Romans are going to nail me to wood, I wonder if it was all worthwhile. I lost touch with my family years ago, and the only company I've got, as I think about my last day on earth, is my partner in crime, and there's not much love lost between us, I can tell you.

I wonder what it's like to die. I wonder if there's a God. I wonder if there's anything after death. Maybe there's just nothing but peace and quiet – that'd be nice. Maybe there are terrible things after death. Maybe I'll come back as something else.

When the Lord Jesus was crucified, he was hung there between two other men. They were both being executed for crimes. They were thieves. Luke says they were criminals. The Lord was hung between them, maybe because the authorities in Jerusalem wanted to give the impression that this was where he belonged. Crucifixion was a horrible experience of death by torture. It wasn't unknown for victims to hang there for a week, alive but dying. It's a dreadful scene, but also a wonderful scene, because here the very heart of Christianity – indeed, the very heart of God – is on display.

A foundational corruption

Luke is often interested in the crowds that gather around Jesus. He uses them and their reactions to hold up as a mirror for us. Let's look at some of the human reactions in this scene. I'd like to suggest that they show us a corruption that is foundational in the human heart.

Emotion without commitment

As the Prince of Life goes to the cross to die for the sins of the world, a bunch of women begin to raise a mourning wail for him in traditional eastern style. Here's a lovely young man going to be terribly executed and they're giving him a proper send-off. They're full of pity. But this time next week it'll all be forgotten. The Lord Jesus gives them a word about the coming judgment which God will bring on Jerusalem in the future. People won't be wailing for Jesus then, they'll be wailing for themselves. They'll be wishing they were dead, that the mountains would fall on them.

There are always going to be people around who are emotionally moved by a tragic story. Good young men put to death by selfish politicians. Young activists who die in police custody. There are many people who are moved quite deeply by who Jesus is and what he represents. They come to church and go home feeling disturbed and stirred up by what they've heard about this Jesus. But it never leads to commitment. It's sincere but it's superficial.

Next week they'll be getting on with whatever is most important in their lives and they will have forgotten about the King. Missionary Don Cormack saw dozens of Cambodian people profess faith in Jesus in the Thai refugee camps where he worked during the early 1980s. Many of them abandoned their faith when they landed in California, or Melbourne or Paris. They'd been emotionally drawn to this lovely person in this lovely book, but in the end, it was superficial. It was emotion without commitment. There was an outward veneer of Christian living – but the internal citadel of their hearts are unconquered by the King's truth.

What's at the end of the road for people who are emotional but uncommitted? Jesus suggests it will be the severe judgment of God. You had the chance to submit to the King and really surrender to his authority, but your interest in him was only skin-deep.

Blasphemous rejection

The Bible has some very hard things to say about human nature, about the foundational corruption within us. It says that the human heart is fundamentally opposed to God. By nature, we are enemies to the true God. We have attitudes and we speak ideas which are insulting to him. We reject the idea that we are sinful and selfish, and by doing so call God a liar. We imagine that we can be good enough to get ourselves into heaven by our decency and good works, and in doing so we reject the way that God has given us to be saved. We say that the Bible is not the word of God, and we defy God's eternal authority. We live as if God doesn't really matter that much. We think that our happiness and our well-being is more important than the glory of God.

We are by nature blasphemous. It's very common for people to speak about Jesus and the gospel with a sneer. And we read in Luke that the rulers sneered at him, even as he was being crucified.

Until I was 17 years old I was a blasphemer. I used filthy language to talk about God and his Son. I thought it was funny, impressive, and grown-up to use God's name as a swear word. But that wasn't my real blasphemy. My real blasphemy was to speak as though God were irrelevant to my life and to my future.

A demanding spirit

'You saved others – save yourself and us' Here's the naked human spirit, stripped of all its cultural niceties, stripped of all those little courtesies we use. It knows that Jesus has healed the sick, the lame, the blind, the demon-possessed, and that he's raised the dead. Now it demands that he do his stuff and that he do it for me. *'Prove yourself to me by doing what I think you ought to do for me, and I will force myself to be impressed by you.'*

There's something in the human spirit which is quite prepared to see ourselves as the centre of the universe. Things ought to happen for my safety, for my comfort, for my wellbeing. We can be very sophisticated about it, and very civilized about it, but beneath the surface, motivating our words and actions is the demand that the universe work for our personal benefit.

The next time you're angry or irritated with people, and you're engaged in rejecting people, ask yourself if there isn't a demanding, selfish spirit beneath the surface. And maybe you're finding an anger even against God because he hasn't arranged things in your life quite how you thought he should. 'This is what I deserve. This is how I should be treated. This is how things should happen for me.'

These are the foundational corruptions in the human heart. And they're there in all their nakedness at the cross.

A fundamental change

We're told in Matthew's Gospel that the robbers who were crucified with Jesus heaped insults upon him – they were both at it. But one of them experienced a fundamental change.

His realisation

He realised as he looked at Jesus and then at his own heart that he deserved judgment, but that Jesus was entirely innocent.

That's often the first step in someone becoming a real Christian. And it can be a painful struggle. You've always thought pretty well of yourself, but now this Christian message is telling you that you're a sinner whose lifestyle is offensive to God; that you can't please him; that you're under his condemnation.

When you realise that truth about yourself, it can shake your heart to its foundations. I deserve judgment, but this man, Jesus, doesn't. In fact, in this chapter, Luke shows us that the Roman governor, the thief on the cross, and the Roman soldier all pass the same verdict on Jesus – innocent. You'll never become a Christian until you agree with God's verdict on your sinful nature.

His repentance

Repentance is the Bible's word for a change of heart and mind. He stopped blaspheming the Lord and started talking to him with a new kind of heart. He stopped joining with his mate in the insults game and started trying to persuade his friend that this man Jesus was different and important.

We don't know what brought about repentance in this thief, but it was fundamental. You may be struggling with this in your own experience. Perhaps you've been going to Sunday church services, but you've realised that Christianity demands a change of heart. There are some things you'll have to stop doing and others you'll have to start doing. And the cost of not behaving like your old mates is beginning to worry you. But there's no way of becoming a true Christian without that step.

His recognition

There is an extraordinary thing about this passage. A few feet away from this thief is another dying man. He's on the same wood, he's got the same kinds of nails through his flesh, and the

42

same kind of blood is running down his limbs. Above him on the charge sheet are the words: *This is the king of the Jews.* What a king! Dying like this, and everybody around shouting and screaming insults.

But in the sweat and urine and stink of that scene, this thief saw his rightful King, his Lord. He somehow perceived that this King was dying for a great purpose, and that he would one day enter into his kingdom by the power of God.

Perhaps when he uttered the name *Jesus* he knew what it meant. *Jehovah Shua* – **God my Saviour.** Perhaps his Sabbath School lessons came back to him: the Jewish longing for the Messiah, the strange words of Isaiah the prophet about the Servant of the Lord dying like a slaughtered Lamb. Whatever. This thief prayed – *'Jesus remember me when you come into your kingdom. After death, after my death, Jesus do your kingly stuff for me.'*

That's a fundamental recognition. You can't become a Christian without it. *'This dying Jesus is my King and I must come to him in surrender, and trust and ask him to be merciful to me and accept me into his kingdom'.* Trusting Jesus as Saviour means trusting that at the cross an astonishing transfer took place. The punishment your sins deserved, along with that of the dying thief, was transferred to Jesus. He was punished by the justice of God so that you might receive the verdict of 'not guilty'. It's understanding what the prophet Isaiah promised in his 53rd chapter, *'We all like sheep have gone astray ... and the Lord has laid on him the iniquity [sins] of us all'.*

A fantastic promise
Later in the day on that first Good Friday, the robber had his legs broken by the soldiers and he quickly suffocated to death under his own weight. His body was disposed of, but his spirit went into paradise with the spirit of the Lord Jesus Christ.

'Today, you will be with me in Paradise.'

That thief now enjoys eternal life. He is in a place of divine glory, waiting for the time when he will receive a new body in resurrection. The Jesus he died alongside received his resurrection body on the third day, but the thief has to wait along with all the Christian dead until it's time for the King to come back and finish his work.

But... Jesus promised him paradise. Who can promise you paradise on his own authority? What would you think if I stood in the street and laid my hand on the head of random shoppers passing by, saying: *'Verily, I John Tindall say to you, today you will be with me in paradise. I can dispense eternal life to people.'*?

I can't even dispense medicines, let alone eternal life. This is either a monstrous untruth told to a dying thief, or it's a glorious hope for all of us. How do we tell the difference?

Three days after his death on the cross, Jesus demonstrated for all time that he has the authority to dispense eternal life by rising from the grave into immortal life. He said about himself: *'I have authority to lay down my life and authority to take it back again'*. He was proved to be the Son of God **with power** by the resurrection from the dead.

He can make the same promise to you that he made to the thief. If you realise your true state before God, repent of your wrong doing, recognise that He is heaven's king, speak to him and ask for mercy, submit to his royal kingship, learn to live under the authority of his word, the Bible – you will one day be with him in paradise. It's a fantastic promise.

5 PARDON

Matt Fuller

> But now a righteousness from God, apart from law, has been made known, to which the Law and the Prophets testify. This righteousness from God comes through faith in Jesus Christ to all who believe. There is no difference, for all have sinned and fall short of the glory of God, and are justified freely by his grace through the redemption that came by Christ Jesus. God presented him as a sacrifice of atonement, through faith in his blood. He did this to demonstrate his justice, because in his forbearance he had left the sins committed beforehand unpunished — he did it to demonstrate his justice at the present time, so as to be just and the one who justifies those who have faith in Jesus.
>
> ROMANS 3:21-26

No, I don't mean: 'Pardon, what did you say?' Nor do I mean, 'Oops! Pardon me. I don't know where that came from.' I'm talking about a *legal* pardon; the sort that a judge gives in a courtroom.

A hopeless jury

I've only been into a courtroom once and I was on the right side of the law. I had to do jury service. It was an odd experience. One member of the jury sat listening to her ipod until the judge noticed and threw her out. Another got very excited when 'Exhibit A', a stash of drugs, was presented to the jury. He opened it up; smelt it; put some in his mouth and exclaimed with great experience: 'Hmm, this is really good stuff!' Again, the judge was not amused!

But the main thing I learned in a courtroom was that there is that one moment – the moment when the judge asks the jury: *'Do you find this man guilty or not guilty?'* That moment was terrifying. It's not like on TV. I wasn't even the one on trial but the reality of punishment was very sobering. The bloke who was on trial in front of me didn't receive a pardon. When he was declared guilty, he broke down and cried.

All of us have an instinctive desire for justice to be done and we all get angry when it's not. We want the guilty punished and the innocent pardoned and set free. Yet, sometimes, the law gets it wrong.

There's the celebrated case in law of Joseph Samuels. Back in 1803, in Sydney, Australia, he was convicted of murder and sentenced to be hanged. On the first attempt to hang him, the rope snapped. Joseph was a big bloke, so they went and got a thicker rope. On the second attempt to hang him, the rope snapped again. So, again, they fetched a thicker rope. On the third attempt, he swung there, quite peacefully, while all those watching got bored. The judge wanted to get home for his dinner, so he declared: *'Since you have proved immune to capital punishment, I grant you a pardon.'*

Now, where's the justice in that? It was good for Joseph that he received a pardon, but I imagine the family of those he killed were outraged and angry. The definition of a proper pardon would be something like this:

> **Pardon:** the forgiveness of a crime and the penalty associated with it. A pardon is granted when an individual is shown to be wrongly convicted or the debt to society has been paid.

So what? Well, the Bible is clear that all of us are guilty and in need of a pardon. Not from a bored little judge in Sydney but from the King of the whole universe. We need a pardon from God for the crimes we've committed and, because he is gracious, he provides a way for that to happen.

'But, no one judges me!'

Often, when I tell people that God views them as guilty, they get angry. I hear comments like: 'How dare you make me feel guilty? I determine what's right and wrong. You're just going around trying to make people feel guilty! I don't care what God thinks about me.'

The problem with that is that we *do* care.

We spend much of our lives wondering what other people think of us. All day long we look for other people's approval of our work, our clothes or our reputation. We hunger for the approval of others. When we do a bit of work for our boss we wonder: 'will he like it or hate it?' We want his approval. We see it's true when we're with our mates: we enjoy their company because we know they like us. There's a sense in which we live life as a series of mini-trials. What will he make of me? Will I be successful?

The reason for this is that, deep down, we want the approval of our Creator. If there is no almighty power judging us then what we do is insignificant. We need God's approval of our lives. So, when people get angry with the idea of God being a judge, I often reply:'Don't tell me that you don't want to know about God's verdict on your life. You do. You can try and ignore him but you'll spend your whole life chasing the approval of others.'

So we all want to know God's pardon for our lives. Let me ask three questions about this:

1. Why do we need God's pardon?

The simple answer is: *because we're guilty of a crime*. The part of the Bible at the start of this chapter tells us: *'for all have sinned and fall short of the glory of God.'* All of us; without exception.

Now 'sin' is a familiar word but sometimes people get a bit confused about what it means. For example, when I tap the word 'sin' into the BBC website, the top three hits I get are:

- 'Sin City' the video game *(I've never played it)*
- a women's hour debate on 'living in sin' *(I've never listened to it)*
- a recipe for Hoi-Sin Duck *(I've never cooked it)*

Most people tend to think that sin is like the middle one: it's the little mistakes we make; the occasional lapses that are a bit naughty but not too bad. Yet the Bible says it is something far worse – it is a mutiny and rebellion against God.

We have rebelled by turning away from God and refusing to recognise his rule. You and I are guilty of revolution against God.

Some revolutions are arguably justified, eg: people who rise up and overthrow a wicked ruler who was governing out of self-interest and committing human rights abuses. That is understandable.

But why rebel against a perfect, loving king?

The more a ruler is lovely, honourable, just, wise and powerful, the greater the crime of rebellion.

And as God is infinitely lovely, honourable, just, wise and powerful, our crime is infinitely wicked. We're stupid to think we can get away with it.

A foolish rebellion

A few years ago, the tiny East Sussex hamlet of Ashurst Wood declared itself independent from the rest of the UK. The People's Republic of Ashurst Wood Nation State (PRAWNS for short) announced its break from taxation and British oppression on 1st January 2000. A revolutionary committee informed the Queen and Tony Blair of its intention to rule 'unencumbered by the law of the land'. They were serious!

They wrote a constitution, they organised checkpoints on the road to nearby East Grinstead (the most likely route of invasion) and they placed a retired army colonel in charge of their defences.

They issued passports and demanded that 'foreigners' (from out-side the PRAWNS) had visas to enter the village. Eventually, though, the rebellion collapsed. Not because the village was invaded but because the bureaucracy was too inefficient. They could not issue visas fast enough to allow the postman, milkman, and delivery lorries into the village. They realised that 'foreigners' had lots of things that the PRAWNS needed.

Now that was a pathetic attempt at independence and no one took it seriously. What about us?

Well, our attempt is equally pathetic.

God sustains us. He provides all that we have. But, unlike Ashurst Wood, our rebellion is serious. We've attempted a bloody coup against the ruler of the universe. We've foolishly thought that we can mock the One who gave us life. We've recklessly taken all the good things that the Creator has given us but then spat them back at him.

The result is that he is rightly furious with us. We've committed a horrific crime and, one day, we'll stand before him in his court-room. He will judge us and his judgment will be terrifying.

Please, don't go into his courtroom without a pardon. The living God doesn't make poor judgments. He is the righteous judge whose justice is perfect.

Why do we need a pardon? Because we're guilty of a dreadful crime and we're facing an awful punishment.

2. How can we get God's pardon?

We know that we should be convicted. How can we be pardoned without an abuse of justice? Verse 25 is the key here:

'God presented him as a sacrifice of atonement, through faith in his blood.'

What does that mean? Simply put, God's just fury at our rebellion is taken by Jesus Christ. We are facing a God who is furious with us, but Jesus Christ came and took the punishment which should be ours.

The trial of Jesus appeared to be a complete miscarriage of justice. Here was a man who was evidently innocent. His opponents couldn't make a single charge against him stick. He knew himself to be innocent, yet willingly died upon a cross. Why? To save people like you and me.

Our only hope lies with this one man.

Despite the formula becoming a little tired, I'm still hopelessly addicted to the TV show *24*. I was very struck by the trailer to season six. Amid dramatic explosions and grand music, the words that appear on screen run like this:

'Threat will rise...
Fear will grow...
Our only hope lies with one man...
For America to survive...
Jack Bauer must die.'

The point of the trailer is that, in order to save the life of millions of Americans, the innocent Jack Bauer must be sacrificed. He is presented as a wonderful hero, nobly sacrificing himself for the good of the many. This sort of heroism is an echo of the ultimate hero – Jesus Christ.

He took the punishment that we deserve so that we might receive a pardon – the forgiveness of a crime and the penalty associated with it. Our only hope lies in trusting that he died instead of us. Or to make it personal, your only hope when you stand in God's courtroom lies with this one man. You need to trust that Jesus died to take your punishment.

Justice is done

Sometimes people say: 'Hey, but that's not fair! How can there be justice when criminals (us) are not punished?' The answer is that the debt has been paid.

If we trust in Jesus' death for us, then we enter God's courtroom with a pardon and we have Jesus as our lawyer to plead our case. It's not that Jesus comes before the Father in heaven and says:

'Come on, you owe me. I died for others, have mercy on this man.' There wouldn't be much comfort in that, because God the Father may decide not to have mercy. Rather, Jesus comes before the Father and say: 'This man is guilty but I have made payment. I do not ask for mercy. I ask for justice.' The Father replies: 'Yes. That's the plan that we created together in order to show both justice and love.'

So, how can we get a pardon? God himself, Jesus Christ, has taken the punishment that we deserve for rebelling against him. Isn't that wonderful? Here is the God who is perfectly loving and, if that isn't enough for you, whatever do you want from God?

3. What difference does God's pardon make?

Where do I begin?! If you come to trust in Jesus, he will turn your life upside down! There are a million and one benefits to becoming a Christian. Let me mention a couple under the heading of confidence.

Confidence in the future

Here is the more important of the two. If you trust in Jesus, your debt has been paid. There is no possibility of being punished. This is like being on trial but already having the pardon in your hand. On day one of the trial, the judge leans across and whispers in your ear: 'This is going to be grim. You're going to hear overwhelming evidence against you. The jury will find you guilty. Yet you'll walk away free because your sentence has already been served. I have already written your pardon in the blood of Jesus. Your debt has been paid.'

Some find this very difficult to understand. Many people have a spiritual deafness and still assume that they can earn their way into heaven. Deafness is dangerous! I read recently of a farmer who went to the doctor suffering with earache, but emerged having had a vasectomy! It was reported like this:

> Brazilian Valdemar Lopes de Moraes was suffering from muffled hearing and thought his name had been called out in the waiting

room at a clinic in Montes Claros. He promptly went into a consulting room where a doctor was performing vasectomies. Asked why he did not complain, Mr de Moraes told staff he thought his ear inflammation had spread to other parts of his body!

Don't be deaf to why this is so important. If you stand before God without Jesus and demand justice on the basis of your own life, you have no hope. If you go with Jesus and plead justice because he has paid your debt, you can have absolute confidence that the Father will welcome you.

Sometimes I'll meet people and ask them: 'Are you a Christian?' A common response is: 'I'm trying?' I suspect these people have no idea of what being a Christian is all about.

You see the Christian says, 'I'm guilty. I deserve punishment. But Jesus has paid that punishment. There is no crime for me to answer for!' If you believe this is true, then you know that you'll spend eternity with God in glory. The trial is over.

Confidence in the present

To be honest, I've short-changed you a little bit with all this talk of pardon. If we trust in Jesus, we get something far better than just a pardon. We get 'righteousness'. That's what the last part of the passage in Romans is saying.

You see, when Jesus swapped places with us on the cross, it's not just that he took our punishment, we also got his perfection. When the Father looks down upon us, he doesn't just see a man who is pardoned. He looks down upon us and sees stunning manliness; perfect obedience; loving devotion. He looks down upon us, sees us wrapped in his Son and loves us. He loves us with the passion with which he has loved his Son for eternity.

My favourite picture of this comes in the film *Chariots of Fire*. There is an obvious contrast between the two leading characters in the film, Harold Abrams and Eric Liddle. At one point, Abrams explains why winning the Olympics meant so much to him: 'When that gun goes off I have ten seconds to justify myself.' Here is a man desperately seeking approval. Success in the race means the acclaim of a nation. Failure means he is a nobody. In a sense, every time he ran a race he was entering a courtroom, waiting for the verdict to come: are you important or insignificant?

By contrast, Eric Liddle explains why, as a Christian, he wants to run: *'God made me fast and when I run I feel his pleasure'*. Here is a man who knows the approval of God. It gives his life joy. He is free from seeking the approval of others and that transforms his life.

So, do you understand what it means to be pardoned? We need it because we're guilty. We get it by trusting that Jesus has paid the penalty for us. The difference is a life of confidence because the God of the universe has already passed judgment upon us.

If you're not persuaded, let me ask you a searching question: *why wouldn't you want this to be true?*

6 | A FACT OF LIFE

William Taylor

Early on the first day of the week, while it was still dark, Mary Magdalene went to the tomb and saw that the stone had been removed from the entrance. So she came running to Simon Peter and the other disciple, the one Jesus loved, and said, "They have taken the Lord out of the tomb, and we don't know where they have put him!"

So Peter and the other disciple started for the tomb. Both were running, but the other disciple outran Peter and reached the tomb first. He bent over and looked in at the strips of linen lying there but did not go in. Then Simon Peter, who was behind him, arrived and went into the tomb. He saw the strips of linen lying there, as well as the burial cloth that had been around Jesus' head. The cloth was folded up by itself, separate from the linen. Finally the other disciple, who had reached the tomb first, also went inside. He saw and believed. (They still did not understand from Scripture that Jesus had to rise from the dead.)

Then the disciples went back to their homes.

JOHN 20:1–10

Building, knocking down and rebuilding office blocks is a never-ending process in London. Recently, demolition began on the London offices of the French bank *Crédit Agricole*. The building was originally constructed by first building a central lift shaft and then adding each floor, one after the other, from the top down. Because of this unusual construction, the engineers have had to dismantle the building from the bottom up. All that is left now is the top seven floors of empty offices still hanging from the central lift shaft while the bottom seven floors have gone. It is an extraordinary sight that looks like a vast game of Jenga!

There was a time when, in spite of the missing bottom seven floors, there was still one working office on the 14th floor of the building. The light was on, and you could see a bloke sitting at his desk, computers running, pictures on the walls, and so on.

Now I suspect that in reality this was the site office. However the person who told me the story told it as if the poor man on the 14th floor was somehow blissfully unaware of what had been going on below him. The world had changed, there was a new future being constructed; yet he kept travelling in to work each day, as if nothing had changed!

In chapter 20 of John's Gospel, we are going to look at the resurrection of Jesus from the dead. We are going to see that, if it happened, it is a unique event that has massive implications for our lives. For us to go on living as if Jesus' resurrection has not happened is as bizarre as working in an office on the 14th floor when all reality below has changed forever.

But first, we should examine the evidence for Jesus' physical resurrection from the dead, so that we can determine whether the claim stands on solid ground.

The evidence

Looking at the evidence, we can see that Jesus' resurrection was unexpected, carefully recorded and repeatedly predicted. It was physical, logical and credible.

It was unexpected

One of the striking things about the independent accounts of the resurrection is that Jesus' disciples didn't expect it. Sometimes we hear people saying that the disciples came up with the story of the resurrection to fit in with what they expected to happen. All the eye-witness accounts we have, however, show us that the very opposite is true.

We can see it from John's account. Mary sees the empty tomb and immediately thinks that the body has been stolen. *'They have taken the Lord out of the tomb, and we don't know where they have laid Him'* she says. Similarly, we find John and Peter unsure of what had happened: *'They still did not understand from Scripture that Jesus had to rise from the dead.'* And again when some angels spoke to Mary: *'They asked her "Woman why are you crying?" "They have taken my Lord away," she said, "and I don't know where they have put him."'*

In Luke's Gospel we find the same reaction from two disciples who met Jesus on a road leading to Emmaus. *'In addition, some of our women amazed us. They went to the tomb early this morning but didn't find his body. They came and told us that they had seen a vision of angels, who said he was alive.'* (Luke 24:22-23) The very last thing they were expecting was to find Jesus risen from the dead. So it's clear that the disciples didn't think Jesus would rise.

With Jesus' crucifixion, all their hope was lost. They gave up. It was only Jesus' appearances to them after his resurrection that finally convinced them.

'Doubting Thomas' is another classic example. In John's account of Jesus' life, we read that the disciple Thomas declared:

'Unless I see in His hands the mark of the nails, and place my finger into the mark of the nails, and place my hand into his side, I will never believe.' John 20:25

In each case, however, having seen Jesus (or at least the empty tomb), they are convinced and their eye-witness evidence is then carefully recorded.

It was carefully recorded

Look again at the passage from John printed at the start of this chapter. Here, we read about the events with such detail, accuracy and precision that it can only come from someone who was actually there.

> They ran... he stooped to look... he saw... one did not enter... the
> other did... there were the cloths... the face cloth was separate...
> the other entered... they believed.

I have a number of friends who work in the legal world. Again and again, they tell me that these accounts read as the eye-witness accounts of those who were actually there. The level of detail and number of incidental observations demands that we see this as eye-witness material.

In addition, all of the accounts of Jesus' resurrection carry minor variations and different observations. Once again, that is precisely what a legal mind would be looking for as evidence of genuine eye-witness testimony. This is no stitch up!

It was repeatedly predicted.

Jesus spoke of his approaching resurrection many times before his death. The disciples, however, wouldn't believe it until they had actually witnessed his risen body. As they reflected on his resurrection, they remembered how Jesus had repeatedly told them he would rise. But it wasn't only Jesus who predicted his death and his resurrection. His resurrection is frequently spoken about in the first part of the Bible – the Old Testament.

It is clearly referred to in 2 Samuel 7, in Isaiah 9, in Isaiah 53, in Daniel, in Psalm 16 and in the book of Hosea. It is also alluded to in a number of other books written over a period of thousands of years. This is what John is referring to in chapter 20 when he writes: *'They still did not understand from Scripture that Jesus had to rise from the dead.'* (John 20:9)

The resurrection of Jesus was unexpected, carefully recorded and repeatedly predicted. But the evidence for the resurrection of Jesus doesn't stop there.

Jesus' resurrection is physical, logical and credible

The eye-witnesses to Jesus' resurrection go to great pains to point out that what they saw was not simply some spiritual experience, still less an hallucination. We read in John's account in verse 20: *'He showed them his hands and his side'*. We read that Thomas said to them:

> "Unless I see in His hands the marks of the nails and place my hand into His side, I will never believe it."

Finally, we read:

> A week later ... Jesus came and stood among them and said... to Thomas, "Put your finger here... and put it into my side."

Furthermore, Luke tells us that Jesus said:

> see my hands and my feet, that it is I myself. Touch me and see. For a spirit does not have flesh and bones as you see that I have. And when he had said this, he showed them his hands and his feet. And while they still disbelieved for joy and were marvelling, he said to them "have you anything here to eat?" They gave him a piece of broiled fish, and he took it and ate before them. **Luke 24:39-43**

This is not a ghost. It is a real physical presence. Any psychiatrist will tell you that hallucinations simply do not happen repeatedly and before a variety of witnesses like this. Jesus has risen physically from the grave.

Jesus' resurrection is *logical*. It is the only logical explanation for the missing body. There was an empty tomb – of that there is no doubt. But no-one was able to produce the body. The obvious thing for the Jews or the Romans to do to have stopped the rumours would have been to produce the body. No one could have claimed Jesus had risen if they could see his body. But the authorities weren't able to do this.

Five hundred people claimed to have seen Jesus risen. Of those 500, many were prepared to go to their death rather than deny what they had seen. The only logical explanation is that their testimony was true and reliable.

The physical resurrection of Jesus from the grave also makes sense theologically. Throughout the Gospels, Jesus claims to be dying to pay God's judgment for sin. God's punishment of human rebellion is death; the wages of sin is death. So, if Jesus died to carry God's judgment for our sins, the inevitable next step is that he would rise physically from the dead. It is logical!

The resurrection of Jesus is also *credible*. There were sceptics at the time who did not believe. They needed to see the clear, hard facts before they would be persuaded. I like to think of Thomas as an immovable Yorkshireman. If we were making a film, we'd have to portray him as a Geoffrey Boycott figure; stubborn, resilient, impossibly hard to persuade.

We can see this side of Thomas' character in verse 25: *'Unless I see in His hands the marks of the nails and place my finger into the mark of the nails, and place my hand into His side, I will never believe.'* However, the man who would not be moved meets the risen Jesus eight days later and, as Jesus commands Thomas to reach out and touch him, Thomas exclaims: *'My Lord and My God!'*

On 21 January 2007, a hunter in Florida shot a ring-necked duck. Believing the duck to be dead, he left it in his fridge at home in Tallahassee. Next morning, when his wife opened the fridge, 'Perky', as she has become known, lifted her head and quacked!

They rushed Perky to the local vet where she underwent extensive surgery. Sadly, mid-way through the operation Perky's heart stopped. The vet struggled to bring Perky round but she stopped breathing. David Hale, the vet, turned to the hunter and his wife and announced solemnly: 'I'm sorry, she's gone.' At that point Perky raised her head from the operating table and began flapping her wings!

That is what is known as *resuscitation*; reviving from apparent death. What happened to Jesus though, was not resuscitation, but physical, bodily *resurrection* – one who was dead rising again.

The evidence stacks up. Jesus' resurrection was unexpected, carefully recorded and repeatedly predicted. His resurrection was physical, logical and credible.

So what does it mean?

The implications

There are two implications of the resurrection of Jesus from the dead. First, it means that *Jesus alone is Lord of all life*. Thomas calls it right in verse 28: *'Thomas answered Jesus, "My Lord and My God!"'* That has to be so.

God shows us in the rest of the Bible that his chosen King will be appointed both Lord and Judge and given all authority over every nation; this King will have God's absolute authority to rule over an everlasting kingdom. The Bible promises that this King will defeat death and reign forever.

As Jesus says:

'As the Father raises the dead and gives them life, so also the Son gives life to whom he will. The Father judges no-one, but has given all judgement to the Son that all may honour the Son just as they honour the Father. Whoever does not honour the Son, does not honour the Father' **John 5:21-23**

Jesus has risen. It is the first day of the week. It is a new beginning for humanity with Jesus ruling in all his God-given power.

This is certainly the conclusion drawn by the earliest Christians. The apostle Paul, preaching in Athens, said that God has

'has set a day when he will judge the world with justice by the man he has appointed. He has given proof of this to all men by raising him from the dead.' **Acts 17:31**

In the Crédit Agricole building in London, before it was pulled down, there used to be a scale model of the new Leadenhall Building that is to replace it. It was a picture – a snapshot – of the brand new future. You could go and see it, walk around it and get an idea of what it was going to be like; a 240m high, glass and steel structure, 48 floors with 12,000 square feet per floor.

The resurrection of Jesus is a picture of the future. Jesus Christ is Lord. He has been given all God's authority. He is God's anointed King and Ruler. Every person who has ever lived will ultimately bow to Jesus and be judged by him. This is a reality – whether we like it or not; whether we believe it or not.

The second implication of Jesus' resurrection is that *Jesus alone can give life*.

In another statement in John 20, Jesus speaks about the possibility of a new relationship with God that begins now and stretches forever into his new future.

In verse 17, Jesus says:

> Do not hold on to me, for I have not yet returned to the Father. Go instead to my brothers and tell them, "I am returning to my Father and your Father, to my God and your God." **John 20:17**

Notice the way that Jesus refers to his disciples as 'my brothers'. He speaks of God as 'my Father' and 'your Father'; 'my God' and 'your God'. In other words, the death of Jesus, that brings the possibility of our sins being forgiven, enables Jesus to call his followers 'my brothers'; and the death of Jesus, that pays for our sins, allows us to call God 'my Father'. Jesus is speaking of a new, close and open family relationship between disciples of Jesus and God himself; a relationship which will extend beyond death to the eternal kingdom of Jesus.

I hope you will allow me to write about myself for a moment. I didn't get started as a Christian until I was an adult. Until then I had always thought that Christianity was about being religious. My understanding was that the Christian faith was all about being good: about rules and regulations; about strange rituals and religious activities in buildings with people dressed up in unusual clothes!

It was only when I was an adult that someone explained to me that the heart of the Christian faith is all about a relationship with Jesus, in which Jesus' death and resurrection brings forgiveness from God, that enables me to become a member of God's family.

Jesus, through his death and resurrection, opens up the chance for us to live with God – both for this life and beyond. We've already seen that, through his death, he claims to pay the price for our rebellion against God and, through his resurrection, that the price really is paid. Once risen from the dead, Jesus announces to his disciples that we can be called 'my brother/sister' by him, and that we can call God 'my Father'.

To know my Creator as my Father, and to be brought into a right relationship with the one who knows me through and through has been, for me, like stepping out of the February gloom into the mid-May sunshine. It has given significance, purpose, direction and meaning to every second of my life. Best of all, it has meant knowing that I am forgiven and loved by God. This is life now as God intended it to be lived. But this way of living extends beyond this life and it means that Christians have great certainty and assurance about life beyond death.

Many years ago, archaeologists excavated some catacombs under Rome. They found some tombs of the earliest Christians, many of whom had died from the most horrific persecution. They had been buried alongside their unbelieving, non-Christian neighbours. The writing on the tombs of atheist and Christian are a compelling contrast which powerfully illustrates the fresh assurance and confidence that the death and resurrection of Jesus brings.

The skeletons of the Christians bear the marks of appalling torture: heads are severed, ribs and shoulder blades broken, bones frequently carry marks of carbonation from burning. In spite of this suffering, the inscriptions speak of peace, joy, triumph and life.

'Here lies Marcia, put to rest in a dream of peace.'

'Lawrence, victorious in peace and in Christ.'

'Being called away, he went in peace.'

But the pagan tombs have none of this hope.

'Once I was, now I am not, I know nothing about it, and it is no concern of mine.'

Jesus' resurrection reassures his followers that death has been defeated; that a new relationship as part of God's family has started; that nothing can separate us from God our Father. He has given us life with him for eternity.

We need to be clear here that no other religious leader has ever made such a claim, and no other religious leader could possibly deliver on such a claim.

Mohammed died in 632 AD in the arms of his favourite wife. His tomb is in Medina. It is possible to visit it. He does not offer forgiveness of this sort and he certainly cannot deliver on life.

Gautama the Buddha died, aged 80, in peaceful serenity surrounded by his devotees.

Confucius died in 479 BC, aged 72, in his home town of QuFu.

Richard Dawkins, Christopher Hitchens, Philip Pullman, the materialistic dream... none of these things offer us what Jesus offers – a relationship with God as Father, and life everlasting as forgiven members of his family.

Some religious leaders offer a 'life' now. But there is none of the rich joy and fulfilled relationship with the living God that Jesus alone brings. Only Jesus has defeated death, paid the price of sin and made possible a union with God, as a privileged member of his family in his eternal kingdom.

It is worth thinking back to our friend sitting up there alone on the 14th floor with the building being demolished beneath him. As I have thought about him, I have wondered what it would take to bring him down. I guess one would want to take him gently by the arm and walk him around the building site, saying: 'Look, my friend, at the evidence. Do you not see the precarious nature of your existence – clinging on as if the future is going to be the same now that everything is changed? Look at what you are missing out on. Look, at the extreme danger of your situation.'

I wonder what it would take for him to change his mind.

I wonder what it would take for you to change yours.

TWO MEN, TWO DESTINIES

Rico Tice

There was a rich man who was dressed in purple and fine linen and lived in luxury every day. At his gate was laid a beggar named Lazarus, covered with sores and longing to eat what fell from the rich man's table. Even the dogs came and licked his sores.

The time came when the beggar died and the angels carried him to Abraham's side. The rich man also died and was buried. In hell, where he was in torment, he looked up and saw Abraham far away, with Lazarus by his side. So he called to him, "Father Abraham, have pity on me and send Lazarus to dip the tip of his finger in water and cool my tongue, because I am in agony in this fire."

But Abraham replied, "Son, remember that in your lifetime you received your good things, while Lazarus received bad things, but now he is comforted here and you are in agony. And besides all this, between us and you a great chasm has been fixed, so that those who want to go from here to you cannot, nor can anyone cross over from there to us."

He answered, "Then I beg you, father, send Lazarus to my father's house, for I have five brothers. Let him warn them, so that they will not also come to this place of torment."

Abraham replied, "They have Moses and the Prophets; let them listen to them."

"No, father Abraham," he said, "but if someone from the dead goes to them, they will repent."

He said to him, "If they do not listen to Moses and the Prophets, they will not be convinced even if someone rises from the dead."

LUKE 16:19-31

My father spent the whole of his career, 38 years, working for a tobacco multi-national. He retired in 1988 and by that time the medical consequences of smoking were increasingly alarming. So how did I feel about this? Well, on the one hand I was very proud of all my dad had achieved in his career, but on the other I was aware of the devastation of lung cancer.

In recent years though, I have begun to feel less uneasy about my father's career. I'm not trying to justify it, but I don't feel particularly guilty because of what now appears on cigarette packets: 'Smoking kills', 'Smoking when pregnant harms your baby.'

I think that gives people a pretty clear warning. It allows people to make an educated choice as to whether they smoke or not: an option which past generations did not have. The only question a person has to ask today is: "Well, do I think this warning is trustworthy? Is it reality or is it a lie which doesn't apply to me?"

A blunt message

'Smoking kills' is a very blunt message and, similarly, Jesus could not have been more blunt in Luke 16. He had to be. It's a red-hot parable, not least because of who he first told it to.

Just before Jesus tells his story, we read that 'The Pharisees, who loved money, heard all this and were sneering at Jesus.' They were meant to be religious people but in their hearts there was a great love for money and an indifference to the poor. So Jesus tells them this story about two men and their two destinies. It's not meant to be history but, nevertheless, this parable, like the warning on a cigarette packet, points to some chilling realities, which we ignore at our peril. The question is: What do you make of it?

What do you think of this story? Do you think it describes reality, or am I just trying to ruin your day?

Two men

So, examining the warning on the packet of this parable in more detail, we see first that we have two different men. The first is phenomenally wealthy, clothed in purple and fine linen. He feasts sumptuously every day. He's got the most fashionable clothes money can buy, and not a day passes without some splendid banquet being held. So, to translate this into London today, it would be suits from Savile Road, shirts from Jermyn Street, ties from Harrods, breakfast at the Savoy Grill, lunch at Simpson's, tea at Claridge's, dinner at the Dorchester.

The word 'gate' in verse 20, is not like the gate of my basement flat – a little side gate. It's a huge ornamental feature. The gates of this rich man's house are like the gates at Buckingham Palace, designed to impress us that the person inside is important. Prosperity oozes from this chap; his clothes, his food and his house. He seems to have a great life.

However, the time comes when the rich man dies. In the afterlife Abraham says to the rich man: *'Son, remember that in your lifetime you received your good things.'* This man had not a problem in life. He had no longings, no worries, no troubles – until the day he died.

The second man we meet could not have been more different. Jesus paints a picture here of abject poverty; as extreme as the rich man's opulence. We read that *'At his gate was laid a beggar named Lazarus, covered with sores.'* The word 'laid' here is far too gentle, it's more liked sprawled. Lazarus is lying there to face the sneering contempt of passers-by. He has no fine clothes on his back, instead his back is covered with sores, perhaps from chronic malnutrition. He's constantly hungry, *'longing to eat what fell from the rich man's table. Even the dogs came and licked his sores.'* The rich man's dishwasher eats better than he does. The only compassion he receives is from mangy mongrel dogs who licked his sores. This man seems to have nothing compared with the rich man. There is one thing, however, that the poor man has which the rich man hasn't. It's something so profound we could easily miss it. This poor man has a name – *Lazarus*.

This is the only time in Jesus' parables that he gives anyone a name. A name means that you're known; you're picked out; you have significance. Lazarus' name in the Hebrew is '*Eliazar*', which is literally 'he whom God helps.' So Lazarus knew God and was known by God. He didn't blame his misfortune on God but in his trials, Lazarus looked to God and put his hope in him. He said:*'God, everyone else has deserted me but I know you and you know me.'* His pain didn't result in resentment which severed his relationship with God; rather, it caused him to trust in God. I think that's why I've never suffered – because God can't trust me with suffering as God can trust Lazarus with suffering. When he suffers, this poor man just goes on trusting in God.

The question which emerges as we examine these two men – one incredibly wealthy but with no identity, the other utterly destitute but known by God – is which of these two men would you rather be? We're presented with two very different men and, as we read on, Jesus draws back the curtain and we can glimpse into eternity and see their two very different destinies.

Two destinies

> The time came when the beggar died and the angels carried him to Abraham's side. The rich man also died and was buried.

It's at this point in the parable when everyone dies. We read that *'The time came.'* Note here the brevity of life. The Bible says we're like a mist that appears in the early morning and, as soon as the sun gets up, it dissolves. Or we're like chaff, which is thrown up and blows away. Life is brief. It's like water which spills onto the ground and can't be gathered back; that's how quickly it disappears. It's like a dream in the night which is forgotten at the breakfast table. The Bible says our life is like a sigh, and it's gone. It's like a breath and it's over. Psalm 90:12 is so striking:

> Teach us to realize how short our lives are. Then our hearts will become wise.

This came home to me recently rather chillingly when I opened up an email sent to me by a friend from an insurance company. It was a questionnaire which they send to people they're going to insure. It's called 'the countdown calculator' and you are asked the following sorts of questions: your date of birth, if you smoke, and if so, how many? Do you exercise regularly? On average how much do you drink? Do you eat saturated fats? Are you overweight. If so, how much? How many hours a night do you sleep? You fill it all in and then the countdown calculator gives you your age of death and your date of death. Which is enough to make anyone go for a run before breakfast and have salad for lunch!

Life is brief. The time comes and we realise that it is very, very short. *'Teach us to realise how short our lives are. Then our hearts will become wise.'*

I had to take the funeral of a close friend, Harry, who was one day older than me. I'd never thought that I would stand at his graveside, not even given it a thought. But he had a pulmonary embolism and died, leaving three children. Life is short, but the crucial point here is that it's not the end. Here is one of the big insights of this passage – Jesus teaches us that our personalities survive death in a conscious state. There is life after death; a coffin is not an exitless box.

To say that we can live this life without consequences is a fantasy, according to Jesus. He is absolutely clear here that these two men encountered two very different destinies after death. You may ask: 'Well Rico, how do you know that? How can you prove that?'

The answer is the resurrection of Jesus. Jesus got through death himself and promises that he can get us through as well. I'm saying that this man, Jesus Christ, lived and taught in first-century

Palestine, had a band of followers, was tried in a Jewish and Roman court, was put up on a cross, had a spear put through his side, was taken down, certified as dead, put in a tomb and three days later he was walking around again. And, because he got through death, he can get us through death. The reality is that because Christ rose, the life to come has broken into this life.

Christianity rests on certain facts of history without which it would crumble. Christ rose on the third day; it's datable. We can't strip Christianity of its historical clothing.

He was crucified under Pontius Pilate: true or false? He rose again, true or false? These are absolutely crucial questions to be answered.

I once took the funeral of a young guy called Stuart. I'll never forget visiting him three days before he died. I was sitting with him and suddenly blurted, 'Stuart, what's it like to die?' Good question, don't you think? Pastorally, very sensitive! Anyway, it was out and he looked at me and I could tell he was thinking: 'I can't believe I've asked this muppet to speak at my funeral.' But he looked at me and he said: 'Rico, Christ has risen.' As he looked into death, his trust was absolutely attached to the resurrection of Christ. My question is: is that true for you? Could it be that Jesus is the one that takes us into eternity?

But what does that feel like? What is heaven actually like? Stuart had a favourite verse, 1 Corinthians 2:9:

> No eye has seen, no ear has heard,
> no mind has conceived what God has
> prepared for those who love him.

So think of the best moment you've had in your life. The very best moment you've ever had. Is it the most intimate relationship ever shared or the giddy elation of falling in love? Now take that moment and multiply its intensity by infinity, and its duration by eternity, and that is what heaven feels like. That's what Stuart was focused on as he went to his death. To know that our feelings will at last be looked after when in this life they're so variable. My feelings go up and down according to whether or not I've had a Mars bar. But Christ has risen. That is the future hope; it's guaranteed by the resurrection. Could it be true?

A terrible alternative

Now we turn to the rich man's destiny. We can see what the Lord Jesus Christ, I think the most loving and tender-hearted man that ever lived – says about the rich man's fate. It's tough stuff. What do you think of this warning?

> In hell, where he was in torment, he looked up and saw Abraham far away, with Lazarus by his side. So he called to him, "Father Abraham, have pity on me and send Lazarus to dip the tip of his finger in water and cool my tongue, because I am in agony in this fire."

Jesus solemnly warns us here that there is a place called hell. So to say there is no hell is to say that there are times when Jesus tells the truth and times when he lies. If you remove the truth of hell, the spiritual truth of this parable collapses. If we can't believe Jesus on hell, how can we believe him on heaven?

As I speak at funerals, I want to speak of heaven but I can have no integrity doing that if I don't also speak of a place called hell. At its heart, the Christian faith is being saved *from* hell, *through* the cross, *for* heaven. At the cross we did the sinning and Jesus did the dying – the just punishment for the offence of sin is death and Jesus bore the condemnation and the death we deserve. The wages of sin is death and he took those wages in our place. He bore our sin, he paid our debt, he endured our penalty, he died our death to save us from hell.

How can we get our heads around that? As Jesus was dying on the cross, he shouted: *'My God, my God, why have you forsaken me?'* Not a cry of physical agony, but a cry of relational agony. He's saying, *'God, why have you rejected me? Why have you thrown me out?'*

Let me try and explain that. When I was growing up in Uganda and Zaire, I had two passions -- stamp collecting and butterflies. Both of these hobbies are brilliant in Africa, and both need a magnifying glass. But I soon found, as a little boy of six, that making little things bigger was not all a magnifying glass could do. I found that if you took one of these out into the midday sun in Africa, the possibilities were endless...

You see, you can take a magnifying glass and concentrate the rays of the sun into such a sharp point of intensity that it burns things. Well, imagine if you can, a massive moral magnifying glass through which passes, not the sun's rays, but God's righteous anger at all the wrongdoing in our lives; at the selfishness and the hatred, at the lies and the dishonesty, at the deceit and most of all the way that we've ignored and misused God in his world.

Picture all God's anger focused and coming down through a massive moral magnifying glass with a terrible intensity until it hits one man in one point of history with such agony, that he cries out, *'My God, my God, why have you forsaken me?'* That is how God saves us from the coming wrath. That's how he saves us from hell through the cross for heaven. The question is: *Why?*

And what had the rich man done to deserve this?

What is hell like?

But Jesus has more to teach us. The key word in verse 25 is 'remember.' This is the warning on the packet.

'Remember how you established your reference points, your goals, your aims for self-fulfillment? Remember how you took the gifts of God and ignored the Giver? Remember that poor man? You had the wealth to help not one but a thousand men just like him, to change their lives, and your heart was absolutely hard. You did nothing and just went off for your next dinner.'

The Bible says that if we have no respect for the poor, we have no respect for their Creator. Abraham reminds the rich man how he took all the good things and used them for himself. God's character will not be mocked; he won't be violated. He is saying that sin must be paid for; either at the cross or you pay for it yourself, but it will be paid for.

> Nothing in all creation is hidden from God's sight. Everything is uncovered and laid bare before the eyes of him to whom we must give an account. **Hebrews 4:13**

Now we get to the heart of what sin really is. The rich man says:

> "Then I beg you, father, send Lazarus to my father's house, for I have five brothers. Let him warn them, so that they will not also come to this place of torment." But Abraham replies, "They have Moses and the Prophets; let them listen to them."

The heart of sin is to ignore the message of Moses and the Prophets. This rich man needed forgiveness; he needed to be forgiven for the way he treated the poor man. At the very centre of the message of Moses and the Prophets, Jesus tells us, is himself.

When Jesus appeared to the disciples after his resurrection, we are told that: *'beginning with Moses and all the Prophets, he explained to them what was said in all the Scriptures concerning himself.'* It would have been a great shock to those sneering religious leaders to discover that the message of Moses and the Prophets is the message of the sacrifice of Jesus in death and blood.

But to ignore the message of Moses and the Prophets is not an *intellectual* decision. That's how it's often depicted today; it's just a choice you make. The Bible says no, it's not an intellectual decision; it's a sin – it's the heart of sin. It's saying: 'I don't need the death of Jesus. I'll get into heaven by living a decent life myself. I don't need his death'.

But the Bible says you can be absolutely charming and yet be right at the heart of sin as you ignore the death of Jesus.

God sends his Son to die and we say: 'I don't need it'. And he says: 'Well then, you can pay for your sin yourself because I have given the gift of my son to pay for your wrongdoing; the times that you've ignored the poor'. The question is, will you remember this warning?

The warning
The rich man suddenly realises what is going on and is desperate-

ly concerned for his brothers – he answers from hell:

> "Then I beg you, father, send Lazarus to my father's house, for I have five brothers. Let him warn them, so that they will not also come to this place of torment." Abraham replied: "they have Moses and the Prophets; let them listen to them."

So Abraham says they've been given a Bible. The Gideons came to their school and gave them a Bible; they got given a Bible at confirmation; their granny gave them a Bible. But they never bothered with the Bible – they played golf on Sunday morning.

'But if they have a supernatural experience, then they'll believe it,' pleads the rich man. *'If someone from the dead goes to them, they will repent.'* But Abraham replies, *'If they do not listen to Moses and the Prophets, they will not be convinced even if someone rises from the dead.'* You either listen to the message of Moses and the Prophets about the death of Jesus and his rescue in the Bible, or you don't have hope.

And that's the warning on the packet. Remember, remember, remember. The question now is this: **who are we in this parable?** Do we all have a part to play? And interestingly, in verse 28 you can see who we are. We are the ones still living. *'For I have five brothers. Let him warn them.'* We are the ones whose destinies are still to be decided by what we do with the message of Moses and the Prophets about Jesus. That's how our future is decided.

Please note here that the rich man doesn't want his five brothers in hell with him. A lot of people say: 'I don't mind going to hell, all my friends will be there.' Can I tell you that this guy doesn't think hell is one long party. The reason is that God, when he withdraws his presence from us, withdraws his gifts.

One of those gifts is love, and another is friendship. T S Eliot wrote: 'Hell is the agony of being unable to love or to be loved.' God withdraws both himself and his gifts. Therefore hell, you see, is the agony stemming from the knowledge of an opportunity forfeited; the agony of looking at the warning and thinking: 'Actually I never bothered with it'. Over the gates of hell are written the words 'too late'. There's no mercy left because we've ignored the death of Jesus.

So we must return to the question I began with. *What will you do with the warning?* Will you give time to investigating it? That's the only question. Will you say: 'Well, I'm actually going to get out my diary, and for once, the important is going to actually supersede the urgent. I'm going to make time because I've got to check out this warning, I've got to check out the resurrection, I've got to check out the message of Moses and the Prophets, I've got to see if it's true. If it's not, the sooner I work that out, the better, and I can just let it go. But if it is, then I need to act upon it.' That's the issue.

Is it a loving warning or am I trying to ruin your day?

8 HEAVEN

Pete Woodcock

fter being visited by a Christian minister, an old lady wrote this at the end of a letter to her daughter:

> PS. The preacher came to call the other day. He said at my age I should be thinking about the hereafter. I told him: "Oh, I do all the time. No matter where I am – in the kitchen, upstairs, in the garden – I ask myself: What am I here after?"

Actually, that isn't a bad question to ask, wherever you are: *'What am I here after?'*

There is a dissatisfaction built into us that longs for more. Something deeper and more joyful, permanent and satisfying. We know that there has to be more than what we have – a sense of something bigger and better. A lot of the time we don't know what it is we are 'here after' – it is just a niggle at the back of our minds.

When I was a teenager, I went to one particular party that had everything a young man could desire. But as I went into the kitchen to get another drink, I was almost overwhelmed, just for a few seconds, with questions. 'Is this all there is to life?' 'Isn't something missing?'

One writer describes these experiences and questions flashing into our minds as the music from a distant country where we long to be. But we catch only a few beautiful notes and so we can't quite grasp the tune. It soon vanishes as we get on with the here and now. It's a bit like those brief moments when a smell suddenly takes you back to some great holiday, or a special day in your childhood.

Questions like 'What is the purpose of your life?' are meant to stop us in our tracks and grab our attention, making us think about what we are doing and where we are going.

Now, when you open the pages of the Bible, you see the promise of 'something bigger and better'. A new creation where people become what they were meant to be – heaven. The word 'heaven' occurs about 550 times in the Bible. Sometimes it simply means the sky (the heavens), but it also means the fantastic new world that people long for. So what does the Bible tell us about heaven?

1. Heaven: not clouds and harps

The famous American writer, Mark Twain, once said: 'You take heaven; I'd rather go to Bermuda.' The politician, Lloyd-George, said that heaven scared him more than hell. And I'm sure that the hopes of a lot of people, even those with a more positive view of heaven, can be summed up as: 'Please God, don't take me to heaven yet. I haven't been to the Great Barrier Reef!'

Of course, if heaven is just a shadowy place of clouds and harps, then the only thing good about it is that it is perhaps a slightly better alternative than hell, but nothing more. This saccharine view is not found in the Bible. Far from it! Nowhere in the Bible is heaven portrayed as something less than this world, something dull, like an eternally bland hymn-singing festival with no electric guitars in sight – only unamplified harps!

Instead, the Bible shows that it is this world that has become dull and broken. In our stupidity, we have broken away from the God of light, beauty, reality, vividness, creativity, generosity, relationship and love. As a consequence, this world is dying. It has been vandalised and 'graffiti-ed' by selfishness, human rebellion against God, and death.

And so, God has continually promised to both judge and renew this world. He has repeatedly promised a better world than this one. One Bible passage lists many people who have trusted God through the ages, and says this of them all:

> They were longing for a better country – a heavenly one. Therefore God is not ashamed to be called their God, for he has prepared a city for them. **Hebrews 11:16**

C.S. Lewis' great illustration was that this world and this life are 'shadowlands' and heaven is the reality – not the other way round! There is a place which is really 'home'. Whereas this world is just the shadow of home. One Bible writer describes living in this world as living in a tent – something that can only ever be temporary, and is not our real home at all.

And for those who look forward to arriving at their true home in heaven, the Bible constantly shows what is waiting there for them. Their Father is in heaven; their Saviour is in heaven; their brothers and sisters are in heaven; their names are in heaven (they have title deeds); their inheritance is in heaven; their citizenship is in heaven; their eternal reward is in heaven; their master is in heaven; their treasure is in heaven.[1]

But even more than that – heaven will be where God is experienced fully. In other words, heaven is where God's magnificence is completely revealed – the place of God's glory and the total revelation of his unimaginable splendour. There can be nothing boring or unreal or shadowy about this!

And people will not live in heaven just as spectators of the greatest show in the universe – we are told that the people there will see God's face. The face is the relational gate to that person. When you talk to someone, you talk to their face. The word 'face' emphasises intimacy with God. Imagine two lovers physically apart, only in contact by phone or email, longing for the day

---

1 see Matthew 6:9; Hebrews 9:24; Hebrews 12:23; Luke 10:20; 1 Peter 1:3-4; Philippians 3:20; Matthew 5:12; Ephesians 6:9; Matthew 6:20

when they meet each other 'face to face'. The Bible says: *'You will fill me with joy in your presence, with eternal pleasures at your right hand'*. Everything that now makes us groan will finally be done away with, and in the very presence of God we will find the purest and truest kind of pleasure possible.

2. Heaven: a renewed universe

Again, C. S. Lewis is helpful here. In his book *The Last Battle*, the children see the land of Narnia die forever and freeze over in blackness. Narnia, the place that they had come to know and love is no more. They are filled with regret. But later, as they walk in a fresh morning light in 'Aslan's country' (heaven), they wonder why everything seems strangely familiar. At last they realise that this is again Narnia, but now different – larger and more vivid, more like the real thing. It is different in the way that a real thing differs from its shadow, or waking life from a dream.

The Bible talks about a new creation, but the new creation is actually this old creation made brand new. The picture in the Bible is of creation waiting to be renewed. In fact, this world is so looking forward to becoming the next that it is groaning. But although the world groans with pain, these are not death throes but birth pangs. The world doesn't groan because its time is short – it groans because of its hope for the future. This world is looking forward to a new birth, where all the broken stuff will be washed away and renewed.

We are told there will be no tears there. God will *'wipe away every tear from their eyes'*. There will be no tears of misfortune, tears over lost love, tears of remorse, tears of regret, tears over the death of loved ones, or tears for any other reason.

We are told there will be no death there. The greatest curse of human existence will be no more. *'Death has been swallowed up in victory'*. Both Satan, who has the power of death, and death itself, will be cast into a lake of fire. There will be no graveyard in this new city of God – only life forever.

3. Heaven: a renewed people

The reason that there are tears, death, suffering, pain and dissatisfaction in the here and now is simply because we have rebelled against God. We have lived life as we want – not as he wants. It's as if we have tried to create a world where we are God, but the trouble is we're not God. We can't cope – we're not big enough. But this isn't just an outward thing. Our rebellion has hardened our hearts and perverted our very nature so that we have become enemies of God.

We all know how natural it is to lie and not be a truthful person. That's because our natures are not in line with God's truth. We all know what it is to feel uncomfortable about what God wants. In fact, the whole business of God and especially the idea that he is speaking to us is something that we want to run away from.

At Christmas a few years ago, I was watching some Christian students do a drama sketch about Jesus in a busy town centre. An old woman, not knowing that I was with the students, said to me: 'Why do they always have to talk about Jesus at Christmas?'

All this is what the Bible calls 'sin'. And we have too easily become used to sin. We can forget just how terrible it is. Haven't you noticed how sin can ruin the best things in life? Everything worthwhile in this world takes effort. There are always thorns and thistles growing in this cursed world that we have to struggle against. There is always envy, ignorance, selfishness, chaos and wickedness – able to destroy in a matter of moments what we have worked a lifetime to achieve. But in heaven people will finally be perfectly free from evil forever. The Bible says about heaven:

> Nothing impure will ever enter it, nor will anyone who does what is shameful or deceitful. **Revelation 21 v 27**

That's a great place! But how on earth could we enter it? 'Nothing impure!' As far as I can see, that excludes all human beings, including me and you. It doesn't matter whether you are the Archbishop of Canterbury or any other supposedly 'holy Joe'! We are still impure. We can all find people that we're better than. But the standard of purity and obedience that will allow us into heaven is not anybody – it's Jesus. How would you feel about being compared with him?

So we've seen the truth about heaven – this fantastic place, this new creation. But how can I get in, dressed in these dirty rags of sin? And with a heart that seems to beat out of tune with God?

Now listen to the greatest truth on earth. From the central throne of heaven itself, a rescuer has been sent – the only one who could make us fit for heaven. Jesus came down to reclaim people, to remake them, to forgive them and purify them. He did all that on the cross. It was there that he swapped places with us. He took our rags of sin and disobedience, and therefore he took God's rejection and judgment. And we know that God has accepted this on our behalf, because after Jesus suffered God's rejection and paid the penalty for our sin, God raised him to life again. See? Jesus has done everything to pay for us the entrance price to heaven.

But even more than that, Jesus sends the Spirit of God to begin to change the very nature of sinners, so that their heart begins to come in line with God. That is why Jesus said that we must be *born again* to enter the kingdom of heaven.

So, for us to get into heaven, it's not just a matter of believing what Jesus has done on the cross – it's experiencing the work of God that begins to change our whole nature. It's not simply a mathematical formula:

Jesus' death + I believe = entrance into heaven.

Rather, when God begins to work in your life, he opens your mind to see what Jesus has done for you, so that you respond in gratitude and worship by the way you live.

God begins to change people in this life, but in heaven his work will be complete. In heaven, people will never again have a single selfish desire. They will never utter hurtful words, or do another unkind deed, or think even one sinful thought. Perfectly liberated from captivity to sin, they will finally be able to do all that is absolutely and wonderfully righteous, holy, and perfect before God.

On earth, people may think they have fully blossomed, but heaven will reveal that we have barely budded. We won't have to hide our talents for fear of pride or making someone else jealous. We will enjoy others' gifts without being jealous ourselves. The things that make living together so difficult on earth will all be gone. People will enjoy relationships that they have never experienced here.

C.S. Lewis tried to explain how much people will be changed in heaven:

> Remember that the dullest and most uninteresting person you talk to may one day be a creature which, if you saw it now, you would be strongly tempted to worship ... He will make the feeblest and the filthiest of us ... a dazzling, radiant, immortal creature, pulsating all through with such energy and joy and wisdom and love as we cannot now imagine.

4. Heaven: are you going there?

Have you thought about the hereafter?

Imagine driving your car without looking through the front windscreen. How suicidal! Who would drive a car without looking ahead – without looking to the future, without seeing what is coming towards you or what you are charging into?

It's hard to imagine someone deliberately doing that because we clearly know the consequences of driving without looking ahead. And yet, in this life the vast majority of blokes are driving along the road and not looking ahead. They have no vision of the future except a few centimetres of education or career or house.

People live their lives mostly looking out of the side window. They live for now – that is what is most important. 'I want everything NOW!' But the problem is that life, like the car, keeps rolling forward. 'Now' is ticking us on to 'eternity'. You will not find heaven here and now.

Mark Twain wrote:

> A myriad of men are born, they labour and struggle and sweat for bread, they squabble and scold and fight, they scramble for little mean advantages over each other. Age creeps upon them and infirmities follow, shame and humiliation bring down their pride and vanities.

> Those they love are taken from them and the joy of life is turned to aching grief ... At length ambition is dead, longing for relief is in its place. It comes at last – the only un-poisoned gift earth has for them – and they vanish from a world where they achieved nothing, where they were a mistake and a failure and a foolishness, where they left no sign that they had ever existed – a world that will lament them a day and forget them forever.

The great news is that it doesn't have to be like this – Jesus has seen to that. But without Jesus, it will be like that, and worse. So, ask yourself: What will be the hereafter for me?

9 THE OPEN DOOR

Richard Coekin

Have you ever regretted neglecting a fabulous opportunity? Not long ago, I was contacted by a South African minister I'd never met before. He said he'd heard about my work and wanted to meet and encourage me and introduce me to his family while he was in London for ten days.

I was fairly busy and thought the suggestion a little intrusive, so I politely explained that I wouldn't really have time — a big mistake as it turned out! He went on to tell me that he was staying with his brother to watch the cricket between South Africa and England at Lord's. He not only knew many of the South African players but his brother was Kevin Pieterson, the England batting sensation, whom he had thought I might like to meet.

I was absolutely gutted. I couldn't possibly declare that I now, suddenly, had time to meet him after all. What an opportunity missed! My sons couldn't believe what a fool I'd been. If only I'd explored a bit further before rejecting his invitation.

I guess most of us can recall turning down an invitation to a party, match or concert and then later feeling devastated on hearing how fantastic it was. Or perhaps we were offered an exciting job or investment opportunity which we now kick ourselves that we refused. Most missed opportunities don't matter too much, but in the following famous passage from Luke's Gospel, Jesus compared his offer of a relationship with God to a wonderful invitation that many people will deeply regret ignoring... forever.

> Then Jesus went through the towns and villages, teaching as he made his way to Jerusalem. Someone asked him, "Lord, are only a few people going to be saved?"
>
> He said to them, "Make every effort to enter through the narrow door, because many, I tell you, will try to enter and will not be able to. Once the owner of the house gets up and closes the door, you will stand outside knocking and pleading, 'Sir, open the door for us.' But he will answer, 'I don't know you or where you come from.'
>
> "Then you will say, 'We ate and drank with you, and you taught in our streets' But he will reply, 'I don't know you or where you come from. Away from me, all you evildoers!'
>
> "There will be weeping there, and gnashing of teeth, when you see Abraham, Isaac and Jacob and all the prophets in the kingdom of God, but you yourselves thrown out. People will come from east and west and north and south, and will take their places at the feast in the kingdom of God. Indeed there are those who are last who will be first, and first who will be last."

LUKE 13:22-30

Jesus was on his way to die! Luke sets the scene for us by telling us that Jesus was *'teaching as he made his way to Jerusalem'*.

This was not a leisurely stroll along the country lanes of Palestine, talking about the wildlife. All the Gospels record that Jesus was on his way to the capital, knowing that he would be arrested, tortured and brutally killed before rising to life forever.

He was constantly explaining to his followers, and to the crowds who gathered wherever he went, why he was surrendering to such a gruesome end. He would offer himself as a sacrifice to suffer what we deserve for the way we treat God and other people. He would do this because he loved us, passionately.

Many people struggle to understand why God, the supreme being, could possibly want to become a man. It seems bizarre that the Creator should shrink himself down to live as an ordinary tradesman from Galilee. So Jesus was always teaching that, just as God's prophets had promised for centuries, God had become an ordinary man to swap places with ordinary people like us. Let me illustrate.

In November 1997, a cargo ship, *The Green Lily,* got into trouble in treacherous seas shortly after leaving Lerwick harbour in Scotland. The lifeboats were unable to rescue the crew in such mountainous waves and so the winchman from the Air Sea Rescue helicopter operating from the Shetland Islands, performed an heroic rescue. Bill Deacon, 27 years in the service, lowered himself down onto the deck of the stricken vessel. There, one by one, he tethered each of the ten crew to the winch and they were lifted to safety. But before Bill Deacon could himself be rescued, he was swept off the deck by a huge wave and immediate lost from sight in the raging sea. His body washed up on shore a few days later. For such amazing sacrificial bravery in the rescue of ten lives, Deacon was awarded the George Cross.

I think such a sacrifice helps us understand what Jesus Christ was doing when he died on the cross. He came down from heaven to earth to rescue us. He sacrificed himself in suffering the penalty due to us for the wrong in our lives, so that we can be free from it and accepted up into heaven. He swapped places with us on the cross. But such love is so surprising that he was having to explain it to people as he walked into Jerusalem to die. Then someone asked a rather stupid question.

An irrelevant question?

Some questions are vital and Jesus was famous for his brilliantly perceptive and often witty answers. But this question is strange:

> Someone asked him, "Lord, are only a few people going to be saved?"

It's a conceptual question of no real importance – like standing on *The Titanic* as it is sinking, and asking the Captain to estimate how many people will survive! It's also an evasive question – speculating about other people. And it's actually quite pointless – after all, what difference does it make? The real question is whether the person asking the question will be saved. But asking questions can sometimes be a screen for avoiding doing something.

Shortly after leaving school, a friend and I thought it would be cool to go parachuting. So we went up to an airfield near Nottingham and joined a weekend parachuting course for beginners.

We heard loads of frightening stories about parachuting accidents and, when it came to the scheduled jumps, we were all pretty nervous. As we were getting into a tiny little plane, which seemed to be made of cardboard, I was suddenly given a new gas-operated reserve parachute that I hadn't seen before and was told that everything was fine so long as the red light was on.

When we'd risen to 2500 feet for the first jumps, the engine was cut, the door in the plane was slid open and the instructor called us all forward to hurl ourselves out of the plane. Suddenly, I was stricken with questions. As I came to the door of the plane I began asking about the reserve parachute. After listening to a few anxious questions, the instructor just thrust me through the door in a tangled heap. The descent was a fantastic experience, although the instructor's report of my jump reads, rather cryptically: '*De-arched and kicking*'!

I had been asking endless questions to try and put off jumping and I needed a bit of a push. I think that's a bit like what was happening here. Jesus was asked an irrelevant question and he didn't bother answering it. Instead, he effectively gave the questioner a big shove. I wonder if we sometimes need the same treatment. One way of avoiding the need to trust in Christ is to try to convince ourselves of the need for delay by asking increasingly irrelevant questions.

Jesus compares eternal life with God to being at a great feast. Picture a glorious banquet with tables piled high with fine food and wine; enormous lobsters, massive steaks, huge raspberry pavlovas, Chilean reds and Old Speckled Hen – you get the picture? A wonderful party being thrown by God for all his true friends. And there's a doorway into the great banqueting hall that is currently open.

Jesus is describing the times in which we still live today. By his own death and resurrection, Christ has opened the door into a wonderful eternity with our generous God. Anyone can be rescued by Jesus' death on the cross, and go in to be friends with God forever. But this door of opportunity will not always be open to us. Jesus has some sobering truths for those who are reluctant to go in.

There's a door that will one day be closed!

The great news of the Bible is that, because of Jesus, the way to God is open to everyone. However wicked we have been in the past, the door is wide open and God is inviting us in. But...

> He said to them, "Make every effort to enter through the narrow door, because many, I tell you, will try to enter and will not be able to. Once the owner of the house gets up and closes the door, you will stand outside knocking and pleading, 'Sir, open the door for us.'"

This door is 'narrow'. I think Jesus means that you can't just drift into God's presence with your family or friends without noticing. You have to search for a narrow door, just as we have to search for the truth about Christ because God wants us to understand how his Son's sacrifice made it possible.

And a narrow door is not an easy door to go through – you can't carry bags of stuff with you. In the same way, entering the presence of God is costly. We have to leave our dependence on other things behind and go in alone. So going through this narrow door is something we must consciously decide we want to do. But we don't want to wait too long, because...

This door will be closed

Jesus seems to be saying that the opportunity to enter eternal life with God will end one day, either because we walk on and ignore the open door or because we die, and then it's too late. Jesus is warning about the 'last-minute syndrome'. You know – leaving things to the last minute.

I have to admit that I have a reputation for the 'last-minute syndrome'. The sad fact is that I love getting on a train when it's already moving, being the last passenger to get on the plane or buying presents just before the shops close on Christmas Eve. But I have also discovered that you can get this approach to life drastically wrong.

When I worked as a lawyer in London, the senior partner in the firm had a box at the Royal Albert Hall, which he let juniors use from time to time. So, although I am not very cultured, I booked the box and invited loads of mates to come with me for a laugh. We went for a drink and a meal beforehand and I guess we were a bit casual about the time, assuming, like many arrogant young men, that nothing could stop us having a great time.

But when we piled out of the taxi outside the Royal Albert Hall two minutes late, we rushed up to the doors where a man in a uniform barred the way. We tried the usual sweet talk: 'Come on, let us slip through quietly – no-one will know and we won't make any noise'. But, all to no avail. Eventually, exasperated by our badgering, the man raised himself up to his full height and declared: 'Sir, this is the Albert Hall, you are too late and the door is closed. Now go away!'

Truth is, I was utterly humiliated. Last-minute syndrome isn't always clever. Yet many people treat God like that. 'I'll think about him later...when I'm old... or desperate... or never,' they say. Someone else put it like this: 'Too many people plan to think about God at the 11th hour and then die at 10.30!'

It's true. In my job as a minister I have buried many people.

It always struck me as extraordinary that, when I have sometimes gently asked an elderly person in their nineties burying their husband or wife: 'Do you ever think about God or life beyond the grave?' I get an answer like: 'Oh no dear, much too busy really'. At 96!

It's clearly a mistake to imagine that we'll ever have more time for God. In the end, we make time for what we really care about and, as we get older, we get more skillful at delaying the subject. It's worth asking how God feels about being treated like this – like a door-to-door salesman we just want to get rid of.

Jesus is warning us all to beware the last-minute syndrome. How tragic to arrive at the doors to the banquet in heaven and hear the sombre words: 'Sir, this is heaven, the door is closed and you are too late!' Jesus is warning that God does not have to hang around waiting until we feel ready to pay him some attention, and the door certainly won't be open when we've died. The door is open now – but one day it will be closed, and then it will be too late.

There will be many unable to enter!

It's quite common to redesign God in our imagination to make him like Father Christmas – a jovial ineffective chap who welcomes us all, and tolerates what ever we do, and feels jolly privileged if we should ever give him our attention. But Jesus is warning that one day, when the door is finally closed with all God's true friends inside enjoying the party, that suddenly everyone will be trying to get in.

Life without God and all the good things that he provides was never going to be much fun. An eternity without friendship, love, joy and kindness would be like living in a permanent nightmare – Jesus called it 'hell'.

Pleading will be useless

Sadly, while many will want to cry out: 'Sir, open the door', they will only then realise that, having lived lives that neglect and insult God, they cannot expect to be with him forever.

Imagine two teachers, James and Jonny, arriving in London for their first posting and looking for somewhere to stay. Searching the *Evening Standard,* they come across a stunning advert:

> Luxury Mansion in Chelsea in ten acres of garden estate, ten reception rooms, pool and wet rooms, eight bedrooms, stables, tennis courts and state of the art cinema, for £10 a month!

Assuming this is an error, the young teachers ring the number and discover that this amazing offer is true. A glorious mansion for £10 a month!

It turns out that the owner is a Russian billionaire who doesn't need the money, but is looking for responsible tenants to take care of his lovely estate while he is abroad on business for the next three years. The only thing the owner asks is that the guys stay in touch concerning the property – respond to emails, report any issues – generally stay in contact.

Well, the two men are ecstatic. They move in and take one floor of rooms each. But they turn out to be quite different. James, who lives on the top floor, is quite the party animal. Within a week, the all-night parties and endless friends moving in have brought cigarette burns on the antiques, beer stains on the walls and vomit on the carpets. The whole place is trashed and everyone knows that, when the owner returns, James will be out on his ear.

Jonny is very different; a disciplined and well-behaved man. He keeps regular hours, polishes the brass door-handles every night, waters the plants every day and licks the windows clean every weekend. Everyone thinks that he is such a polite and responsible young man that the owner will surely let him stay forever. So they are shocked when the owner returns and throws both men out onto the street.

To anyone who bothers to ask, the owner patiently explains: 'I know that James trashed the place and that Jonny was better behaved, but they treated me the same in different ways. Neither of them responded to my messages and requests. Both of them completely ignored me as if I wasn't there. Although Jonny was polite and well-behaved, it was plain that they both thought me an idiot and both treated my generosity as nothing. It's not the amount of mess they made, but the way they treated me that matters most – and they cannot stay any longer.' That seems fair to me.

I tell this story to explain how we treat God in different ways. We live in God's world, enjoying his many kindnesses. Some of us trash our lives, leaving wrecked relationships everywhere, and we know we are in serious trouble with God.

But others of us are very polite, well educated and moral, and are surprised to hear there's any problem. But in our hearts we all treat God like dirt. We usually ignore him except when we want something. The rest of the time we criticise and accuse him for the wrongs brought into the world by humanity, and then demand that he give us his heaven forever. We are much mistaken.

God is not obliged to welcome any of us. Indeed, it is incredible that he has sent his only Son to open the front door for us again. If we spend our lives ignoring the opportunity that cost Jesus the cross to open that door for us, we can hardly complain if we are left out forever.

Familiarity is not the same as friendship

Jesus also warns that vague acquaintance with God is not the same as real friendship. When people respond: 'We ate and drank with you…you taught in our streets', Jesus seems to have in mind those who are familiar with him but have never joined the people of God at the party.

One can imagine a Londoner saying: 'But God, we went to church events – especially at Christmas and weddings – we ate and drank with you … and we heard some sermons and we like your book – you taught in our streets'. But God will say: 'I don't know you' – we're not really friends, are we?

I was once painfully reminded of the difference between real friendship and mere acquaintance. Some years ago, I met an

England rugby player, Rob Andrew, at a drinks party. Rob now has an important role in the England Rugby administration. We chatted a fair bit and I enjoyed my brush with celebrity. A few months later, when I was studying in Sydney, Australia, I heard that the England team would be practising at Sydney University's training ground before playing Australia so I went down to watch them.

At one point, Rob was practising his kicking and came over to where I was watching from the sideline. I called out: 'Rob, how are you?' expecting him to be moderately excited to see me, a friend of his. But when he looked in my direction, he just stared straight through me. He didn't remember me at all and just carried on practising. I felt about two feet tall.

How ridiculous of me to think of myself as a friend – I was merely an acquaintance.

What would Jesus say to us if he returned today to gather all his friends together for the great party in heaven. If he turned up at church, you can imagine him walking down the aisle and greeting the astonished congregation. To many he would be saying, 'How good to see you my old friend! Good to see you too. I know how hard it's been for you and, yes, great to see you both, I've prepared everything for you. You're going to love it and oh...' As he stops by your chair, what will he say to you? Sadly, to many he will have to say: 'No. I don't know you, do I? We're not really friends, are we? I'm sorry but it's now too late. I'm afraid you can't come with me now.'

How tragic to have assumed we were close friends when, in truth, we were no more than vague acquaintances. Familiarity is not the same as friendship.

There'll be anguish among those left outside

Jesus was the kindest and most loving man that ever lived, but he says these hard things because he loves us and because we can be so stubborn, proud and lazy. He doesn't want any of us to be left outside, so he tells us how dreadful it will be.

> There will be weeping there, and gnashing of teeth, when you see
> Abraham, Isaac and Jacob and all the prophets in the kingdom of
> God, but you yourselves thrown out. People will come from east and
> west and north and south, and will take their places at the feast in
> the kingdom of God. Indeed there are those who are last who will
> be first, and first who will be last.'

Jesus says 'there will be weeping there' as people are overcome
with anguish and regret. There will be 'gnashing of teeth', which
sounds odd but is describing the desperate realisation of the eternal consequences of ignoring Christ. This will be worsened by the
recognition that God's people will all be with him.

Christians from all nations will be in heaven

'Abraham, Isaac and Jacob and the prophets' are the people of God
in Old Testament times. No surprises there then. *'But you yourselves thrown out,'* says Jesus. Why didn't I pay more attention to
that Christian friend who kept trying to get me on an evening
course exploring Christ?

*'People will come from east and west and north and south and take
their places … in the kingdom of God'*. Because, even if currently in
Britain, churches are emptying or Christ doesn't seem too popular in our circle of friends, that is not the picture around the
world. It's never sensible to determine truth by democracy, but it's
helpful to realise that in South America and Africa and Asia millions and millions are turning to follow Christ, even if the deca-
dent west is currently in rebellion.

And, before we start to feel superior, Jesus warns: *'there are those
who are last who will be first, and first who will be last'*. Those who
seem successful in the world, the privileged, wealthy, powerful
and comfortable, who assume they have no need of Christ, will be
astonished to find themselves excluded from God's heaven.

Some of us may have had such privileged lives that we find it
almost impossible to believe that we are not God's favoured elite,
but have been left out forever. But many who have had little priv-
ilege in life, and have been well aware of their faults and failings,

have turned to Christ for salvation and will be welcomed into heaven forever.

Could we be left outside, weeping? How tragic would it be to be awakened from our graves to realise that we are outside heaven, gazing in at the crowd gathered in God's presence, champagne glasses in hand, enjoying God's eternal party? How heart-breaking would it be to see a daughter talking to our wife, or a friend talking to parents and asking: 'Why isn't he here? I thought he would be here. Why isn't he here, mum?' And to hear the tragic reply, 'I'm afraid that your dad could never really be bothered with God. I did try but he always said he was too busy' or 'I'm afraid he had lots of intellectual questions and doubts – but he didn't really want to hear them addressed in case he had to change his lifestyle so he just ignored all my invitations. It's very sad.'

Imagine being outside the closed door, in the darkness with the weeping crowds, filled with regret and anguish at all those missed opportunities. So what does Jesus advise?

He says: *'Make every effort to enter through the narrow door'.*

Make some effort while the door is still open. Go in and get to know Christ before it's too late and the door is closed. Go to a church that explains the Bible clearly. Join an evening course that provides answers to the questions you might have. Pray in your heart that God will help you to know him.

And, as soon as you can, become a Christian. Go in though the door to get to know God. You begin this relationship with a prayer of commitment to him. We don't have to know everything before we go in. It's a bit like getting married. I didn't know everything about my wife before we got married. I'd have many years to get to know her. But I knew enough to know I didn't want to live without her and I didn't want to risk losing her any longer. Same with Christ. We can't know everything when we start out – but we know enough to realise we don't want be without him and we don't want to risk losing him. Here is a prayer we could pray to become a Christian:

Dear God,

I want to enter the narrow door into your presence.

I want to get to know you and to be with you forever. Please forgive me for ignoring and rebelling against you.

Thank you for sending Christ to die in my place on the cross.

Please accept me into your presence to become your respectful friend. Amen

Is there any sensible reason to continue ignoring Jesus' invitation? Why would we want to spend eternity weeping with regret over lost opportunities?

Let me end with a sobering tale. Imagine three demons are training at St Lucifer's college to work for the devil in stopping people coming to Christ for salvation. At their annual review, these three demons were brought before the devil to explain their proposed tactics.

The first demon bowed before Satan and said: 'I'll tell them that there is no God'.

'Hopeless!' shrieked Satan, 'All they have to do is to study Jesus Christ to know that God is real. Get back to stoking the boilers.'

The second demon now fell before Satan to explain his strategy. 'I'll tell them that there is no forgiveness,' he stammered.

'Imbecile!' screamed Satan. 'All they have to do is to study the death and resurrection of Jesus to know that there is forgiveness. Back to stoking the boilers, you fool!'

Finally, the third demon came before Satan with a wicked grin across his slimy face. 'Well, what will you do to stop people coming to Christ?' demanded the devil. 'Oh, it's very simple,' said the smirking demon. 'I'm just going to tell them that there's no hurry'.

'Brilliant,' said Satan with a triumphant smile. 'Get to work immediately'. And he is, everywhere. Even as some of us are reading these words, he is whispering in our hearts: *'There's no hurry...'*

'Make every effort to enter through the narrow door, for many, I tell you, will try to enter and will not be able to.'

WHAT NEXT?

Here are some suggestions:

1. Talk to God

It may be that you've become convinced that you can trust Jesus with your life. You know that you've rebelled against God and have not treated other people as you should. But you understand that Jesus willingly died on the cross to deal with the problem of sin in your life. You want to accept that forgiveness for yourself, and begin an amazing new life following him. If that's you, talk to God about these things. Many people have found that a simple prayer saying *Sorry, Thank you* and *Please* has been the start of a new life with God.

> Lord Jesus, I recognise that you are God
> and have the right to control my life.
> I have rebelled against you, sinning in thought, word, and
> deed, sometimes unconsciously, sometimes deliberately.
> I'm sorry for the way I have lived and ask you to forgive me.
> As best as I can, I want to turn away from rebellion and obey
> you.
> Thank you Lord Jesus, for dying for me on the cross.
> Please come into my life and take complete control of it.
>
> Amen.

If you do decide to begin following Jesus, it's a good idea to tell another Christian so that they can support you.

2. Read a Gospel

You may have already read quite a bit about Jesus' life. But the best way of getting to know him is by reading one of the historical accounts of his life, known as Gospels: Matthew, Mark, Luke or John. Pick up a Bible and turn to one of these short books. A modern translation is best.

3. Join a Course

You may still have lots of questions so why not join a course like *Christianity Explored*? These courses are informal and relaxed. You won't be asked to read aloud, pray or sing. You can ask any question you like, or you can just sit and listen.

Visit www.christianityexplored.org and click on *Find a Course*.

4. Dig deeper

This book only has the basics in it. Other people have written longer books explaining in more detail what it means to be a genuine follower of Jesus. Here are some books that may help
- A Fresh Start *by John Chapman*
- Christianity Explored *by Rico Tice*
- If you could ask God one question
  by Paul Williams & Barry Cooper

Visit the Good Book Company website to order these books or for some further recommendations:

www.thegoodbook.co.uk

More resources for men

A FEW GOOD MEN *Richard Coekin*

What kind of man do you want to be? Who do you admire? Rugged sportsmen, smooth film stars and wild rock musicians all compete for our admiration. But are these men the role models that we should aspire to be?

A Few Good Men presents a series of character sketches of biblical men who faced the same struggles that men still face today: living in an immoral culture, costly decisions, sexual temptation, peer pressure, guilt, fear and worry. A deeper understanding of these struggles will inspire today's men to follow the true hero of this book - Jesus Christ.

9781905564590 | 208pp | £7.00

MAN OF GOD: *a Good Book Guide*

This set of Bible studies, aims to unpack the answers the Bible gives to the question of identity that men face today. We will learn our God-given role in creation and how that has been ruined by the fall. And we will discover how we can start to be restored through the man above all men - Jesus Christ. Some things that emerge will be controversial in our culture, even in some of our churches. This course doesn't set out to be politically correct but faithful to God's counter-cultural word.

9781581342864 | 10 studies | £3.00

FATHERHOOD: *Tony Payne*

In this very readable book, Tony Payne takes a fresh look at what the Bible says about dads. What does it really mean to be a father? What should fathers be trying to achieve? And how can they do a better job? He answers these questions with insight, practical wisdom and good humour. If you only ever read one book on fatherhood, make it this one.

9781876326999 | 189pp | £7.00

DISCIPLINES OF A GODLY MAN *Kent Hughes*

Our churches and homes need men who aren't afraid to work up a 'spiritual sweat.' Using engaging vignettes, scriptural wisdom, and practical advice, Hughes helps you 'train' in the areas of marriage, fatherhood, integrity, prayer, friendship, work, and more. Personal study questions help you apply what you learn.

9781581347586 | 304p | £10.00

MISSING THE POINT *Vaughan Roberts*

Is there a meaning to life? Where are we going? What is the purpose of it all? Is human history a random process going nowhere? Or is it under control - heading towards a destination? And what about my life? How does it fit in? Does it have a point?

Christians believe the answers to all these questions are found in the Bible. It is an ancient book but it is also God's message to us today - a message that focuses on one man, Jesus of Nazareth. *Missing the Point* looks at the most important turning points of history as outlined in the Bible, and considers where we have come from, where we are going and what this life is all about.

9781850787631 | 40pp | £3.00